W9-BRF-631

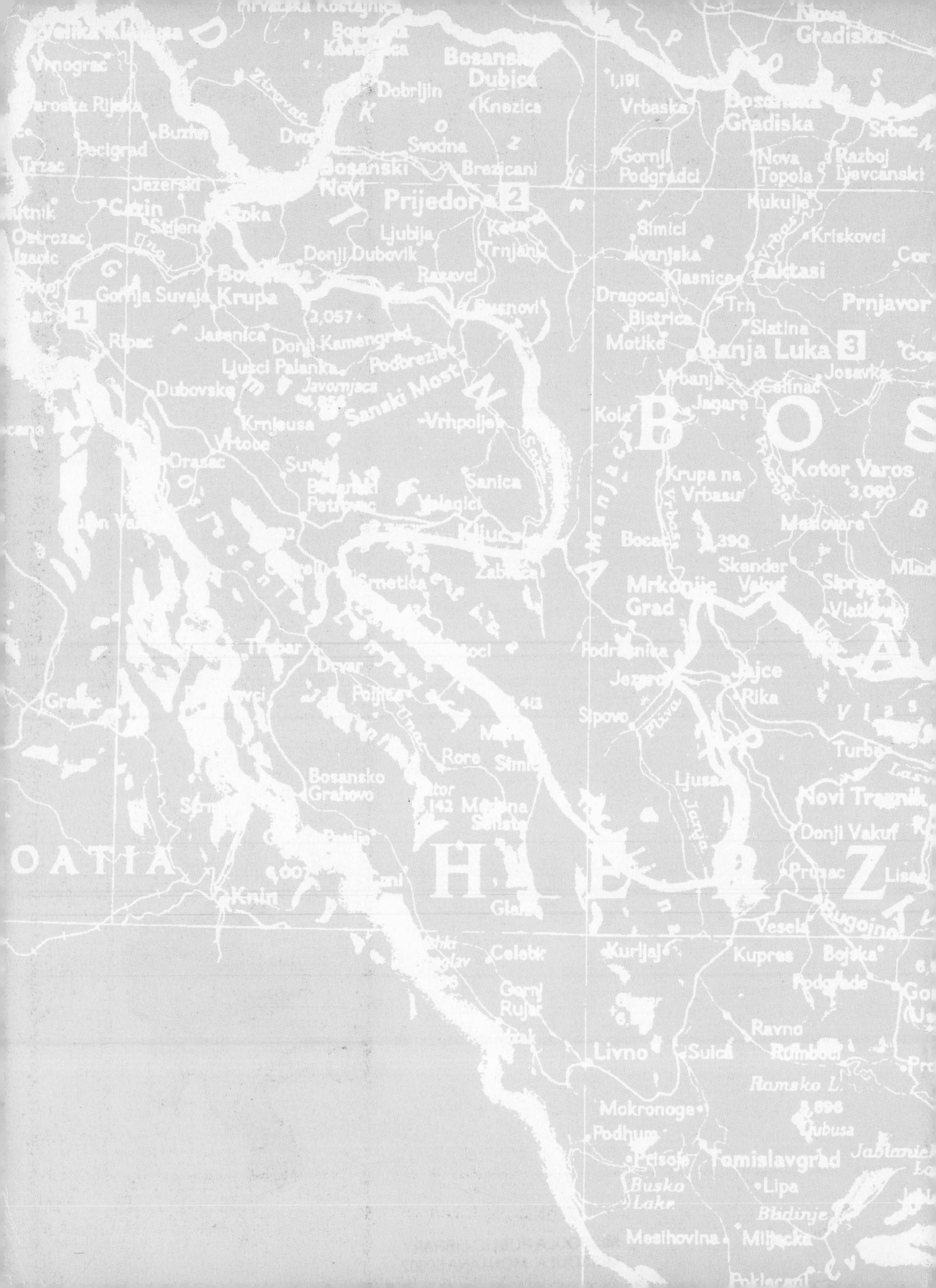

Hrvatska Kostajnica
Bosanska Kostajnica
Bosanska Dubica
Nova Gradiska
Vrnograc
Dobrljin
Knezica
1,191
Vrbaska
Bosanska Gradiska
Buzhin
Dvor
Svodna
Srbac
Pecigrad
Gornji Podgradci
Nova Topola
Razboj Ljevcanski
Bosanski Novi
Brezicani
Jezerski
Prijedor
2
Kukulje
Cazin
Ljubija
Simici
Kriskovci
Ostrozac
Donji Dubovik
Ivanjska
Trnjani
Klasnica
Laktasi
Razavci
Gornja Suvaja
Krupa
Dragocaj
Prnjavor
1
Bistrica
2,057
Slatina
Ripac
Jasenica
Donji Kamengrad
Motike
Banja Luka
3
Ljusci Palanka
Podbrezje
Josavka
Javornjaca
Vrbanja
Celinac
Dubovske
Sanski Most
Jagare
Vrhpolje
Kola
B O S
Krnjeusa
Vrtoce
Kotor Varos
Orasac
Krupa na Vrbasu
3,090
Sanica
Petrovac
Velagici
Kljuc
Bocac
390
Skender Vakuf
Mrkonjic Grad
Trubar
Podrasnica
Jajce
Drvar
Jezero
Rika
Sipovo
Pliva
Turbe
Rore
Bosansko Grahovo
Ljusa
Novi Travnik
Donji Vakuf
OATIA
H E R Z
Knin
Prusac
Bugojno
Vesela
Celebic
Kurljaj
Kupres
Bojsko
Gornji Rujani
Livno
Suica
Ravno
Ramsko L.
Mokronoge
Podhum
Prisoje
Tomislavgrad
Busko Lake
Lipa
Blidinje
Mesihovina
Miljacka

joe kubert

A STORY OF SURVIVAL

fax from sarajevo

coloring * Studio SAF - Pahek
color separations * SAF - ScanArt, Slovenia

DARK HORSE BOOKS

"this book is dedicated to karim zaimovic"

This book is dedicated to a man I've never met.

My knowledge of him extends only to four packets of photographs taken by him in Sarajevo in March 1995. They were sent to me by Ervin to be used as reference, in order that I might gain better credibility in my illustrations of war-torn Sarajevo.

*

Each packet contained thirty or more snapshots. Some were of buildings pock-marked by shells. Debris-strewn streets through which Sarajevo citizens stepped carefully, avoiding charred, crippled cars and mortar holes. Small queues of people waiting outside stores whose shattered windows were held together by tape or replaced by cardboard and plywood. A building whose signs hung limp against blackened stones, letters missing, mute testimony to the haphazard destruction visited here. In one photo, taken of a storefront whose glass window was still intact, the reflection of a man holding a camera. He holds it almost chest high, but does not sight through the viewfinder. Perhaps he doesn't want to call attention to the fact that he is taking these pictures. Perhaps the ever-present snipers would notice and aim at this attractive target.

Ervin has marked descriptions on some of the pictures. "Central Bank," with an arrow pointing to the building. "Marshall Tito Street," on the avenue in front of the building. "Main Post Office," a side view and a detailed double picture of the post office's facade, consisting of windowless, black holes that look like eyeless eye sockets staring sightlessly from the photo. Yet, the four, ornately carved, stone eagles that stand above the main entrance, wings spread as if for instant flight, have not been touched by bomb blast or bullet.

The last photo in one of the four packets is of a young man, obviously unaware that his picture was being taken. He has a partially chewed sandwich in his mouth and is looking to a side, toward us, as if we had just walked in on his quick meal unexpectedly. Under his right elbow is a picture portrait of Jim Carrey in his role of the Riddler, mouth wide open in a crazy grin, hair bright orange-red, eyes discreetly covered by a green mask.

Below the photo is written:

Joe, this is my friend, Karim Zaimovic, a young journalist and big comics-strip fan from Sarajevo, who took all these photographs for you!
—Ervin, May 21, 1995

Karim Zaimovic was in Sarajevo working for a local publication (DANI). He had been promised a job in Ervin's business, now operating in Slovenia. It would mean working in a profession he truly loved, for a comic-book publisher, and a future that would fulfill his every dream.

Karim Zaimovic died of a grenade wound to the head in the streets of Sarajevo in August 1995. He was just 24 years old.

Mike Richardson * Publisher
Bob Cooper * Editor
Brian Gogolin * Book designer
Mark Cox * Art director
Vasja Ocvirk * Editor — SAF

Neil Hankerson * executive vice president
David Scroggy * product development
Andy Karabatsos * vice president & controller
Mark Anderson * general counsel
Randy Stradley * director of editorial
Cindy Marks * director of production & design
Sean Tierney * computer graphics director
Michael Martens * director of sales & marketing
Tod Borleske * director of licensing
Dale LaFountain * director of m.i.s.
Kim Haines * director of human resources

Fax from Sarajevo™

Published by
Dark Horse Comics, Inc.
10956 SE Main Street
Milwaukie, OR 97222

First hardcover edition: October 1996
First softcover edition: October 1998
ISBN (hardcover): 1-56971-143-7
ISBN (softcover): 1-56971-346-4

10 9 8 7 6 5 4 3 2 1

Printed in Hong Kong

acknowledgments

Ervin Rustemagic,
for reliving his two years of horror and, as a result, affording me vital details that must have caused pain to recall;

Debby K.,
for standing guard and deflecting time incursions and permitting me to finish my work;

Bob Bean,
for his interest and perspective;

Bob Cooper,
for his encouragement and acts of inter-communication; and

Muriel K.,
without whom none of this would have been possible.

contents

"Sarajevo's climate is very continental, with a short, hot summer, when nights are still cold due to the constant breeze coming from the surrounding mountains. Winters are rich with snow, from November until April. Snow has been recorded in June — a fact which can be found in old Sarajevo chronicles. War so far hasn't changed the climate. The moon is still shining, the sun rises, rains fall, and it snows, too."

From *Sarajevo Survival Guide*

chapter 1

chapter 2

chapter 3

chapter 4

chapter 5

chapter 6

chapter 7

chapter 8

chapter 9

chapter 10

chapter 11

chapter 12

ervin returns to sarajevo

P. O. Box 844, 7000 AV Doetinchem, Holland
Tel. (31-8340) 35789, Fax (31-8340) 63165

March 21, 1992

Fax to:
MURIEL & JOE KUBERT
Dover, New Jersey

Dear Joe & Muriel,

Although the situation in Bosnia is not clear and calm at all, I decided to go back home and will leave on Sunday morning, by car, together with Butzo, my assistant, who came here two weeks ago to help me finish the last things and pack up for the trip.

We will overnight in Germany Sunday night, and will also have to overnight Monday night either in Austria or Slovenia, to be able to arrive home for the daylight.

Therefore, please, direct all your mail, faxes and/or phone calls (after March 24) to our Sarajevo office:

STRIP ART FEATURES
Georgi Dimitrova 49
71000 SARAJEVO
Tel. (38-71) 455-225, 544-037
Fax (38-71) 46 43 41, Telex 41539 saf

In case you have some communication difficulties and cannot reach us by fax, use the fax number of our Dutch office (31-8340) 63 165. The person in charge of SAF B.V. HOLLAND is Mrs. Ali Magnin-Bulten and she will do her best to forward your fax to us in Sarajevo. The lines between Holland and Sarajevo are usually good.

Love,

ON A NARROW, WINDING ROAD NEAR THE NORTHERN BORDER OF WHAT WAS ONCE YUGOSLAVIA, A SMALL CAR STABS LIGHT INTO ITS PATH TOWARDS SARAJEVO... MARCH 1992.
JOE KUBERT
BY DAYLIGHT TOMORROW, BUTZO...WE SHOULD BE HOME.
NOT SOON ENOUGH, ERVIN. I AM ANXIOUS TO SEE MY FAMILY.
COUGH COUGH
IF YOU DON'T STOP SMOKING SO MUCH, YOU WILL NOT LIVE LONG ENOUGH TO SEE ANY-ONE.
I CAN HARDLY WAIT TO SEE EDINA AND THE KIDS.
I REALLY DIDN'T WANT EDINA TO GO BACK TO SARAJEVO. BUT-- SHE MISSED HER FATHER AND HER BROTHER SO. AND THE KIDS MISSED THEIR FRIENDS...
COUGH, COUGH
YOU ARE A WORRY-WART, ERVIN. I'M SURE EVERYTHING WILL BE ALL RIGHT. THE FIGHTING IS OVER.
IT IS NIGHT...THE OPEL KADET DIESEL THRUMS CADENCE. WINTER RETAINS A LOOSE HOLD ON THE BEAUTIFUL, WOODED MOUNTAINS.
2

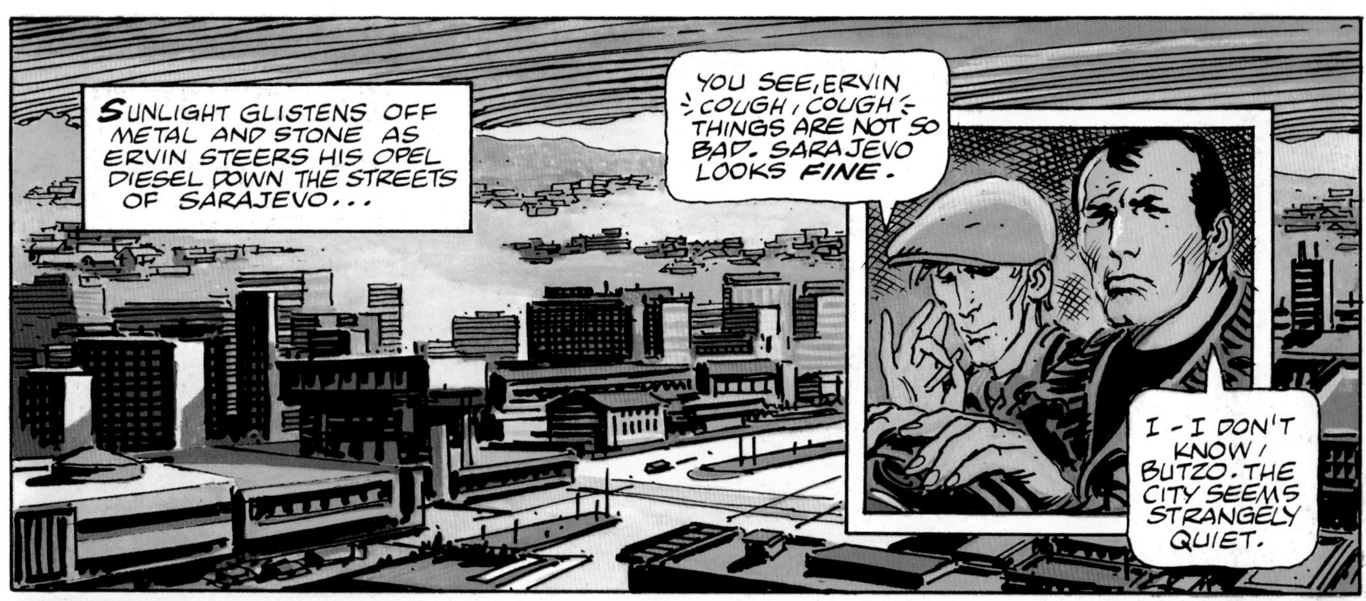
SUNLIGHT GLISTENS OFF METAL AND STONE AS ERVIN STEERS HIS OPEL DIESEL DOWN THE STREETS OF SARAJEVO...
YOU SEE, ERVIN
COUGH, COUGH
THINGS ARE NOT SO BAD. SARAJEVO LOOKS FINE.
I - I DON'T KNOW, BUTZO. THE CITY SEEMS STRANGELY QUIET.

LOOK... IT'S PAPA.
PAPA!
EDVIN.. MAJA!
YOU HAVE BOTH GROWN SO BIG SINCE YOU LEFT WITH MAMA ONLY TWO WEEKS AGO.

I WILL SEE YOU LATER, ERVIN. I'M GOING TO MY FAMILY.
OKAY, BUTZO. SEE YOU LATER.

ERVIN... I - I'M SO GLAD YOU'RE HERE ...WE MISSED YOU.
ME, TOO, EDINA.
HOW ARE THINGS HERE? HAS THERE BEEN ANY TROUBLE?

THERE IS SHELLING OUTSIDE THE CITY. THE SERBS ARE ATTACKING SMALL TOWNS.. FARMS.. BUT, IT'S NOT BAD HERE.. YET.
NO ONE IS SURE WHAT IS GOING TO HAPPEN. I - I AM HAPPY YOU CAME, ERVIN.
3

THAT NIGHT..
EDINA.. WHY ARE YOU UP?
ARE YOU ILL-?
NO, NO, ERVIN. I... JUST CANNOT SLEEP.
A FEELING. I-I DON'T KNOW WH-
SUDDENLY...
KRUMPF
WHUMP
WHRUMPF
WHREEEEEEEEEEE
EXPLOSIONS!
JUST OUTSIDE THE HOUSE!

EDINA! COME AWAY FROM THE WINDOW!
THE CHILDREN-
THEIR BEDS ..ARE EMPTY!
WH-WHERE ARE THEY?
MAJA! EDV-

M-MAMA.. I-I AM SCARED!
IT-IT IS ALL RIGHT, MAJA. WE ARE HERE.

IN BASCARSIJA, THE "OLD CITY," SHOPKEEPERS ARE STARTING TO OPEN THEIR STORES...
...WHEN A BARRAGE OF SEARING STEEL AND FLAME RIPS INTO MEN, WOMEN, AND CHILDREN WITH INDISCRIMINATE SELECTIVITY.
4

EDINA... GET THE CHILDREN'S THINGS. WE'VE GOT TO GET OUT OF HERE—
B-BUT.. WHERE WILL WE GO? THIS IS OUR HOME—
KNOCK KNOCK
ERVIN! YOU ARE BACK! I JUST CAME TO CHECK ON EDINA AND THE KIDS—
THANK YOU, IGOR. YOU ARE A GOOD NEIGHBOR. WE ARE PLANNING TO LEAVE—
NO! I HAVE JUST HEARD ON THE RADIO.. THE ROADS ARE CLOSED!
THE SERBS ARE KILLING ANYONE WHO TRIES TO GET OUT OF SARAJEVO. YOU CAN-NOT GET THROUGH—

THEN.. WHAT CAN WE DO? IF WE STAY HERE THEY WILL SLAUGHTER US..
WE HAVE NO CHOICE, ERVIN.
"THEY ARE STOPPING CARS... ROBBING THEM... BEATING AND KILLING FAMILIES.
"YOU MUST STAY.. UNTIL WE LEARN WHAT WE CAN DO, ERVIN."
5

MR. MILOSEVIC... WHAT WILL IT TAKE TO STOP THE FIGHTING? WHAT DO THE SERBS WANT?
ONLY PEACE. AND THE RETURN OF OUR LAND.
WE ONLY WANT TO PROTECT OURSELVES.. AND TO RULE OUR OWN LAND!
THE MUSLIMS AND THE CROATS HAVE ALWAYS KEPT US SERBS SUBJUGATED.. UNDER THEIR THUMB.
NOW IS OUR TIME TO BE FREE! TO RID OURSELVES OF THE YEARS -- NO, CENTURIES OF OPPRESSION..
..TO CLEANSE OUR-SELVES OF OTHER ETHNI-CITIES!
I NEVER THOUGHT I WOULD LIVE TO BE SORRY THAT COMMUNISM IS GONE. AT LEAST THE CHETNIKS FEARED THE RED BEAR...
...SO THEY DID NOT SHOW HATRED OPENLY!
NOW TERROR WILL STRIKE WITHOUT FEAR OF REPRISAL. ONLY THE UNITED NATIONS -- OR, THE UNITED STATES CAN DO ANYTHING TO STOP THEM.
6

SERB FORCES POUR INTO THE OUTSKIRTS OF SARAJEVO...
COME OUT, MUSLIM DOGS!
DO NOT TRY TO HIDE FROM US.
WH-WHAT DO YOU WANT OF US?
EVERY-THING!

AND YOUR VERY PRETTY DAUGHTER AS WELL.

PAPA! DO NOT LET THEM-
QUIET! I HAVE A USE FOR YOU, GIRL!

ARE YOU ANIMALS? LEAVE HER. LEAVE MY DAUGHTER ALONE!
SHE IS FORTUNATE TO BE CHOSEN... FOR OUR PLEASURE.
SHOOT HIM!

BY THE DIM LIGHT OF A FALTERING BULB, ERVIN'S FINGERS DANCE OVER THE COMPUTER KEY-BOARD...
...TYPING THE MESSAGES BY WHICH HE KEEPS CONTACT WITH THE WORLD OUTSIDE SARAJEVO.
7

Dear Joe and Muriel,
Who would have dreamed that this would happen? It is like a nightmare. The grenade explosions are incessant.
SKREEEEEEEEEE
WHRAAM

Electricity is disrupted periodically. Water pipes are broken. People line up for water rations all day long.

Fuel for cooking is difficult to get. Children are risking their lives helping parents find anything that might burn . . .

Snipers seem to find great pleasure in killing children. Perhaps they do it to get at the adults who run out to help the injured children.

EEROOOOOSHHH
SWOOOOSH

CRACK
TINKLE
TINKLE
KRUNCH

WHY ARE THEY DOING THIS, PAPA? THE AIRPLANES MAKE SUCH A NOISE... WHY?

I-I... DON'T KNOW, EDVIN.

DON'T THEY KNOW THEY FRIGHTEN US? SO WE MUST HIDE IN THE CELLAR.
DO THEY WANT TO HURT US, PAPA?

9

THE THOUGHT OF DEATH IS HELD LIGHTLY BY CHILDREN.

THE CONCEPT OF MORTALITY IS UNKNOWN TO CHILDREN.

THE HAPPY SOUNDS OF CHILDREN AT PLAY ARE A LURE FOR OTHER CHILDREN.

A FUSILLADE OF SNIPER FIRE EDUCATES THE SURVIVORS AND CUTS SHORT A FUTURE NEVER TO BE REALIZED BY OTHERS.

IS A BONUS PAID FOR ELIMINATING A YOUNG LIFE?

WHAT IS THE COST OF A YOUNG LIFE THAT COULD HAVE BEEN ANOTHER PICASSO...

..OR DA VINCI... OR BEETHOVEN? OR YOUR CHILD?
10

c h a p t e r 1

c h a p t e r 2

c h a p t e r 3

c h a p t e r 4

c h a p t e r 5

c h a p t e r 6

c h a p t e r 7

c h a p t e r 8

c h a p t e r 9

c h a p t e r 10

c h a p t e r 11

c h a p t e r 12

war is hell!

Strip Art Features, G. Dimitrova 49, 71000 Sarajevo, Bosnia-Herzegovina
Tel. (38-71) 455-225, 544-037, Telex 41539 saf yu, Fax (38-71) 46 43 41

April 12, 1992

JOE KUBERT, Dover, New Jersey

Dear Joe,

I want you to know that we all citizens of Sarajevo are very, very proud of our several hundred Jewish citizens.

Mr. Ceresnjes, the president of the Jewish community in Sarajevo was on our TV last night to tell the people that it is not true that they escaped from Sarajevo. Namely, all the Serbian press, radio and TV have published the news on Friday that all the Jewish people have escaped from Sarajevo. However, the Serbian press and TV, who are under total control of Milosevic' party, are publishing only lies and they are creating the news which suit their government.

Mr. Ceresnjes said that all the Jewish citizens who are able to work and fight will remain in Sarajevo to defend their city until the last of them lives.

This statement produced tears in the eyes of all our neighbors and all the people I know in Sarajevo. Therefore I wanted you to know that we all are very proud of them. If you could communicate this to the Jewish communities in your states, perhaps they would send a nice note of encouragement to Mr. Ceresnjes.

The situation in Bosnia is very bad and is getting worse and worse every day. The Serbian terrorists, supported by the Yugoslav Federal Army, are making massacres in small villages, especially along the river of Drina which is dividing Bosnia from Serbia.

Also the big cities, like Sarajevo and Mostar, are under constant attack of the Serbian artillery. We don't have much chances to survive unless there will be a fast military intervention from the Western European countries or the United States. The problem is that all the Federal Army forces that pulled back from Slovenia and Croatia are located in the Bosnian territory now, and they are fighting for Serbia, against Bosnian people and against Bosnian government.

There are many Serbian terrorists on the roofs of the high buildings in Sarajevo who are using rifles with sniperscopes to kill people in the street (mainly small children). Two of them were captured by our police and they said on the TV that they were not shooting people for the hate, but for the money. Serbian leaders are paying them $300.– for every bullet which they shoot from the roof, and special bonus for every person they kill.

We can only hope that we will survive all this and that the Serbian politicians, their leaders, army generals, their TV and newspapers' editors will pay one day for what they are doing to innocent people now, and for what they were doing in Croatia in the last month. They are worse than fascists and worse than beasts.

Love,

Ervin

SARAJEVO.
APRIL 1992...
IT IS SUNNY OUTSIDE, MAMA.
CAN WE GO OUT TO PLAY, PLEASE?
PLEASE, PLEASE, PLEASE.
NO, DAMIR-- IT IS TOO DANGER-OUS-
WE HAVE BEEN INSIDE FOREVER. WE WANT TO FEEL THE SUN.
PLEASE, PLEASE, PLEASE. WE WILL BE CARE-FUL.
ALL RIGHT... BUT... STAY CLOSE TO THE HOUSE.
C'MON, ENA. DON'T BE A SCAREDY-CAT. IT'S OKAY-
JOE KUBERT
2

O-DAMIR! ENA!
OH, MY GOD...
M-MAMA... MAMA. THE B-BOMB FELL FROM THE SKY.
IT-IT HURTS..
MRS. KORVAC. WHAT HAP-?
OH, NO.
WE MUST GET THEM TO A HOSPITAL.
BUT... HOW? THE SNIPERS-
M-MAMA...
THE STREETS ARE BLOCKADED!
IF WE DO NOT GET THEM TO A DOCTOR, THEY MAY DIE!

MY CAR IS PARKED DOWN THE STREET.
EDINA... TAKE MAJA AND EDVIN BACK INTO THE HOUSE.
WE ARE ONLY A FEW MINUTES FROM THE BOLNICA DOBRINJA.
STAY LOW, MRS. KORVAC... AND PRAY.

WE ARE IN LUCK, MRS. KORVAC... NO ONE IS SHOOTING AT US.
HURRY, ERVIN... HURRY.
SA★244-196

WHERE IS EVERYONE?
HELP.- I HAVE A HURT CHILD!

I AM DR. HAJIR. IN HERE... QUICKLY. WE HAVE A FULL EMERGENCY ROOM.
OMIGOD. TH-THE CHILDREN.
YES... IT IS TERRIBLE. THIS IS A WAR AGAINST HELPLESS WOMEN AND CHILDREN.

WE ARE RUNNING OUT OF BANDAGES AND MEDICINE.
"I CAN ONLY IMAGINE WHAT IS HAPPENING IN MOSTAR... THE OLD CITY. THE SERBS ARE BOMBING WITHOUT CAUSE OR REASON. EVEN THE OLD BRIDGE THAT HAS BEEN STANDING FOR HUNDREDS OF YEARS IS A TARGET..."
4

"MOSTAR HAS EXISTED FOR CENTURIES... TODAY THE PEOPLE ARE A THREAT TO NO ONE!
"BUT THE SERBS ARE INTENT ON DESTROYING EVERYTHING THAT THEY DO NOT DOMINATE.

"SERB ARTILLERY SHELLS SMASH THE OLD HOUSES... THE SHOPS...
EEEEEEEEEEEEEEEEEEEE
WHRUMPF
"...THE PEOPLE, YOUNG AND OLD ALIKE."
DR. HAJIR... THE CHILDREN ARE CAUTERIZED AND BANDAGED.
GOOD. FORTUNATELY THEIR WOUNDS WERE NOT TOO DEEP.

CHANGE THEIR BANDAGES EVERY DAY.
THANK YOU, DOCTOR.
COME, MRS. KORVAC. WE WILL GO HOME.
5

HOW CAN I REPAY YOU, ERVIN? I HAVE NO MONEY. NOTHING.
DON'T WORRY, MRS. KORVAC. JUST SO LONG AS THE CHILDREN ARE OKAY.
BESIDES...
POSTA

...WE ARE ALL IN THIS HELL TOGETHER.

LOOK HOW THE LITTLE ONES CARRY SO MANY BOTTLES FOR WATER...
...AS IF THEY GO TO PLAY.
THE FAMILIES NEED WATER.

ERVIN! THANK HEAVENS YOU ARE BACK!
HOW ARE THE CHILDREN?
EVERYTHING IS OKAY, EDINA. DON'T LET EDVIN AND MAJA PLAY IN THE STREET.
QUICKLY... BACK IN THE HOUSE. IT IS NOT SAFE OUT HERE.
6

SARAJEVO IS SITUATED IN THE VALLEY OF THE RIVER MILJACKA. THE 1984 WINTER OLYMPICS WERE HELD IN THE MOUNTAINS THAT SURROUND SARAJEVO. BUT—
—THE MOUNTAINS HAVE BECOME HOME FOR SERBIAN TANKS, MORTARS, ANTI-AIRCRAFT GUNS, AND SNIPER FIRE. HOUSES, MUSEUMS, CHURCHES, MOSQUES, HOSPITALS, CEMETERIES, MEN, WOMEN, AND CHILDREN ARE TARGETS.

YET... PEOPLE ADAPT. PLASTIC AND CARDBOARD REPLACE GLASS.

BOARDS AND MATTRESSES REPLACE SPLINTERED WALLS.

COBBLESTONES REPLACE SHATTERED CEMENT.

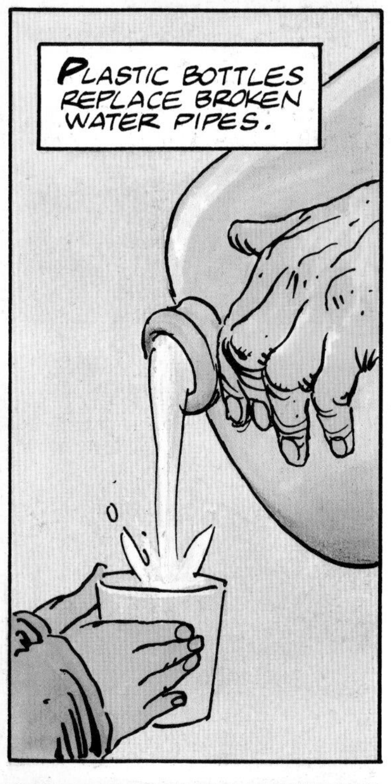
PLASTIC BOTTLES REPLACE BROKEN WATER PIPES.

I HOPE THE ELECTRICITY STAYS ON, PAPA.
WHO IS THAT MAN, ERVIN?
HE IS THE PRESIDENT OF THE JEWISH PEOPLE IN SARAJEVO, EDINA. LET'S HEAR WHAT HE HAS TO SAY...
7

April 14, 1992

Dear Muriel & Joe,

I've tried many times this morning to call the Jewish Center in Sarajevo, but both lines were constantly engaged.

We also hear that the State Department is putting a very big pressure on Serbia, their leaders and the Federal army to stop the war and massacres in Bosnia. But verbal threats cannot help us, because Serbs don't listen to anyone, and they continue to destroy everything that cannot belong to them.

Love, Ervin

YOU MADE IT INTO WORK, BUTZO... GOOD MAN.
NOT SO GOOD, ERVIN... COUGH·COUGH THE BOMBS NEVER STOP.
HOW IS IT IN THE STREET?
YOU NEVER KNOW WHEN OR WHERE THEY WILL LAND.
I BROUGHT YOU SOME CHOCOLATE CANDY... FOR THE KIDS. WE HAD EXTRA.

SO, ERVIN... DO YOU THINK THIS WORK WE'RE DOING WILL EVER BE PUBLISHED?

WE MUST BELIEVE IT, BUTZO... THAT THIS WILL END-- AND THAT WE WILL GET OUT ALIVE--
FOR US.. AND FOR THE CHILDREN.

KRUMPF
WHUMP
THAT WAS CLOSE, ERVIN. IT'S A GOOD THING THESE HOUSES ARE MADE OF STONE AND CONCRETE.
COUGH, COUGH
BUTZO.. IF THE BOMBS DON'T GET YOU, THOSE CIGARETTES WILL! SNIFF
THEY SMELL FUNNY. HEY! THEY'RE NOT-
TEA, ERVIN. CHAMOMILE. COUGH, COUGH THE BEST TOBACCO IN THE WORLD USED TO BE PRODUCED HERE IN HERZEGOVINA.
NOW... WE SMOKE TEA. IT'S A CRAZY WORLD. COUGH
9

13/04 '92 20:11 ☎078 146072 M.LODEW
DEAR JOE AND MURIEL,
WHAT CAN WE SAY ABOUT ERVIN AND HIS FAMILY?
IT'S LIKE THAT BOOK TITLE SOME YEARS AGO-
"BAD THINGS HAPPENING TO GOOD PEOPLE."
IN THE PORT CITY OF DORDRECHT IN HOLLAND, A HAND-WRITTEN FAX IS PREPARED...
I HAD ERVIN ON THE PHONE TODAY. WHILE WE WERE SPEAKING, BOMBS FELL ONLY YARDS AWAY. THEY WERE SITTING ON THE FLOOR OF HIS OFFICE WHERE THEY STAY BECAUSE OF FALLING GLASS.
HERMANN (THE ARTIST) HAS A RELATIVE WHO IS IN THE FRENCH PEACE-KEEPING CONTINGENT OF THE U.N. STATIONED IN SARAJEVO. MAYBE HE CAN DO SOMETHING. LIKE...
...GET HIM AND HIS FAMILY OUT! FULL PLANES (SERBIAN FEDERAL SOLDIERS) FLY IN EVERY TEN MINUTES AND FLY OUT WITH SERBIAN CIVILIANS TO BELGRADE.
...AND, IN SECONDS, IS RECEIVED IN DOVER, NEW JERSEY-- IN AMERICA.
AT THE MOMENT, ONLY SERBS ARE ALLOWED TO LEAVE. TIME OR NEWSWEEK HAS A PORTFOLIO OF PICTURES THAT REALLY SENDS THE HORROR HOME.
LOVE / MARTIN
10

Stop the Butcher of the Balkans

Slobodan Milosevic, strongman of Serbia and wrecker of Yugoslavia, may not be as ruthless and reckless as Saddam Hussein. But his aggression against the newly independent republic of Bosnia and Herzegovina has become just as blatant — and just as urgently requires a stern response. Unless the international community acts against him now, thousands may die.

The U.S. and Euro much to

remnants of the Yugoslav Army, indiscriminately blast round after round into Bosnia's defenseless communities.

The multi-ethnic character of those communities is evident in their skylines. The minarets of Muslim mosques and spires of Eastern Orthodox and Roman Catholic churches stand side by side. Bosnia's people — 44 per

Serbs and 17 percent Cr

SAF fal

Strip Art Features, G. Dimitrova 49, 71000 Sarajevo, Bosnia-Herzegovina
Tel. (38-71) 455-225, 544-037, Telex 41539 saf yu, Fax (38-71) 46 43 41

April 13, 1992

Dear Muriel,

The United States have recognized Bosnia & Herzegovina as an independent country, and many other countries have done that, too. The Federal Army doesn't accept that fact, neither the Serbian leaders accept that recognition . . . Therefore the eyes of most of the population here are concentrated to the U.N. and European Community, hoping for a fast action, otherwise thousands of people will get killed in the next couple of days.

The situation is much more dramatic than anyone can imagine.

At this very moment the Serbian terrorists are holding barricades around here, in our neighborhood, shooting at anything that moves. We're missing food, medical supplies and everything else. The telephone communications are O.K., but we don't know for how long. All the shops are closed.

All the ways out and in Sarajevo are blocked. If you drive your car some place, you risk to be stopped by the Serbian terrorists who will just kill you, or throw you out (if you're lucky) and take your car.

The post offices are all closed and so are the banks. We're in a trap, surrounded by the Federal Army and Serbian terrorists (which is the same thing).

Right now we're hearing cannons who are bombing Sarajevo from the surrounding mountains, as well as a lot of the machine-gun fire. Somehow, we already got used to live with it. The army jets are flying very low over the roofs, breaking the windows with their sounds and threatening people. The jets are not bombing here yet, but they're doing a lot of bombing in and around Mostar (that old city with the bridge which we visited).

Under such circumstances it is quite difficult for Maja and Edina to keep up their English.

If you hear any major news, please do let us know.

Love,

chapter 1

chapter 2

chapter 3

chapter 4

chapter 5

chapter 6

chapter 7

chapter 8

chapter 9

chapter 10

chapter 11

chapter 12

life in sarajevo

* * * edvin is ill

Vijecnica - The national library in Sarajevo was totally destroyed in the beginning of the war.

April 18, 1992

Dear Muriel and Joe,

It is 12 days now as we are suffering from the bombing and disasters that such a dirty war can bring.

You cannot imagine what it means to us to hear from you every day. I have no words to say how much we love you, Hermann, Martin, Jacques and everybody else who cares so much about us and about what's happening here. I wish I could write separate faxes to every one of you every day, but it is very difficult to do under such circumstances.

I am sending you herewith the fax which I sent to Martin and Jacques in Holland this morning.

Love,

MAJA Ervin Edina

April 18, 1992

Dear Jacques and Martin,

The best news which I got in the last two weeks was your fax of yesterday, Martin, in which you're saying: "I'm almost starting to feel optimistic". You are a born pessimist, and it is really very cheerful to hear that from you.

Yesterday was a terrible day here. Serbs have massacred many people in the north of Bosnia, but the worst was in a small village, where people accepted some Serbian refugees in their homes. They have given beds, food and some clothes to the Serbs, and when the Serbs were leaving the village, they cut throats of all their hosts.

We, in Sarajevo, are not too much afraid of the bombing, but we're afraid of what the Serbs have done in other cities and in Croatia, too. They come into people's houses, kill everybody they find there and steal everything they can carry away. In the area of Dubrovnik they were stealing houses in three waves. The first wave was stealing money, jewelry and other valuable things which they could put in their pockets and bags. The second wave of Serbian "soldiers" was stealing computers, TV sets and similar stuff, while the third wave was coming with big trucks stealing furniture, etc . . . In this third wave some of them were bringing their wives along so that they can choose the furniture which they like . . . After the third wave, they were burning and blowing up the houses they robbed.

It snows in Sarajevo today, and nobody knows what this day will bring to us, and how much blood will be spilled over the snow.

Best, Ervin

THE TOWN IS QUIET... OUR GUNS HAVE FLATTENED THEM.
THOSE WHO ARE NOT DEAD HAVE FLED... THE TOWN IS OURS.
JOE KUBERT '94
THEY WILL LEARN THAT WE SERBS WILL NOT STOP UNTIL WE HAVE TAKEN BACK ALL OUR LAND.
GO THROUGH THE HOUSE WITH A FINE-TOOTHED COMB. LEAVE NOTHING OF VALUE.
THEY HAVE NO USE FOR MONEY ...OR JEWELRY.
MY WIFE WILL APPRECIATE THIS RING.
2

I HOPE THIS TELEVISION STILL WORKS.. IT'S A NICE, BIG PICTURE SCREEN.
I FOUND A CLOCK RADIO. A SONY.
GET MOVING. THE TRUCKS ARE PULLING UP.
HOLD IT. THIS ONE IS STILL ALIVE. I'LL TAKE CARE OF HIM...
STEP ON IT! THE TRUCKS ARE PULLING IN FOR THE HEAVY STUFF.
BLOM
SOME MORE FURNITURE. PERFECT FOR MY HOUSE.
BE CAREFUL. DON'T SCRATCH THE FINISH.
DON'T TEAR THE MATERIAL.
ALL RIGHT, ALL RIGHT. LET'S JUST GET IT ON THE TRUCK.
I HEAR THEY HAVE A NICE COLLECTION OF SILVERWARE IN THE NEXT TOWN.
3

MID-APRIL IN BELEAGUERED SARAJEVO... FLAKES OF SNOW SPIRAL AMID EXPLODING SHELLS THAT RIP RESIDENTIAL AREAS.

EDINA AND THE CHILDREN ARE SLEEPING IN THE NEXT ROOM, BUTZO...
THE BASEMENT IS THE SAFE PLACE FOR THEM, ERVIN. COUGH, COUGH.
YOUR MOTHER, ERVIN... HAVE YOU HEARD ANYTHING?

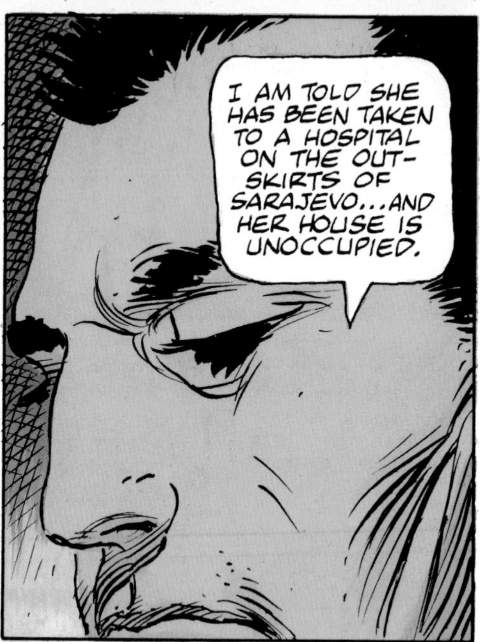
I AM TOLD SHE HAS BEEN TAKEN TO A HOSPITAL ON THE OUT-SKIRTS OF SARAJEVO...AND HER HOUSE IS UNOCCUPIED.

I CANNOT EVEN GET TO SEE HER. THE SERB MILITIA-
EDINA--IS THERE ANYTHING WRONG?
WE CANNOT SLEEP, PAPA... THE BOMBS ARE TOO LOUD.
YOU WORRY ABOUT YOUR MOTHER, ERVIN...

...BUT...WE CAN ONLY DO WHAT IS POSSIBLE. IF YOU ARE HURT... OR WORSE... IT WOULD HELP NO ONE.
"THE CANNONS AND THE SNIPERS DO NOT CARE WHO THEY HIT."
4

ERVIN... I FEEL SO GUILTY. IF I HADN'T INSISTED THAT I AND THE CHILDREN SHOULD RETURN TO SARAJEVO... WE WOULDN'T BE IN THIS SITUATION...
"WHO COULD HAVE DREAMED THAT THIS WAR WOULD HAPPEN...?
"WHO WOULD HAVE THOUGHT THAT SERBS WOULD KILL CIVILIANS? WOMEN AND CHILDREN? AND THAT THE WORLD WOULD LET THEM?
"THERE ARE RUMORS THAT THEY HAVE BUILT CONCENTRATION CAMPS... LIKE THE NAZIS DID IN 1939...
DON'T BE SILLY, EDINA...
"MORE AND MORE WE HEAR OF ATROCITIES AGAINST WOMEN...
"HOSPITALS ARE FILLED WITH CHILDREN... ORPHANED ... CRIPPLED..."
5

AT LEAST WE ARE SAFE... SO FAR.
TAKE THE CHILDREN INSIDE, EDINA... TRY TO GET SOME SLEEP.
ALL RIGHT, ERVIN...
GOOD NIGHT, PAPA.

IT IS **HARD** FOR EDINA... BUT OTHER SARAJEVANS ARE MUCH WORSE OFF.
HEY, ERVIN... I JUST LEARNED OF A NEW RECIPE FOR **POMMES FRITES**.
COUGH, COUGH.
POTATO CHIPS? WHERE DO YOU GET A **POTATO**, BUTZO?
THAT'S JUST **IT**, ERVIN... YOU DON'T **USE** A POTATO. I'LL SHOW YOU...

A LITTLE FLOUR... A SPOON OF BI-CARBONITE... SOME VINEGAR... WATER..
COUGH, COUGH.
I HOPE YOU KNOW WHAT YOU'RE DOING, BUTZO.

NOW I **MIX** ALL THIS STUFF AND KNEAD IT INTO DOUGH...

..THEN..CUT IT INTO THE SHAPE OF **CHIPS**...

...FRY IN A LITTLE OIL...

...AND, **VOILÀ!** POTATO CHIPS WITH-OUT POTATOES COUGH, COUGH.
6

DEE-LICIOUS, EH, ERVIN?
IF THOSE CIGARETTES DON'T GET YOU, THESE POMMES FRITES WILL!
IT'S ALMOST DAYLIGHT, BUTZO. A SHIPMENT OF REAL FOOD ARRIVES TODAY... FROM THE RELIEF ORGANIZATIONS.
YES. AND MAYBE THEY'LL HAVE CIGARETTES.
COUGH, COUGH.

I'LL TAKE EDVIN'S WAGON...
HERE IT IS ALMOST MAY AND WE STILL HAVE SNOW.
IT'S A CRAZY WORLD.

WARM WEATHER WILL BE HERE SOON, BUTZO. BUT... I SHUDDER TO THINK OF ANOTHER WINTER OF THIS WAR.
I NEVER THOUGHT I'D BE USING EDVIN'S CART FOR FOOD SHOPPING.

YOU SEE WHAT A DIET OF POMMES FRITES CAN INSPIRE, ERVIN? LET'S GET IN LINE...
COUGH, COUGH.
WHREEEE
7

B-BUTZO.. ARE YOU... ALL RIGHT?
I THINK I'M... S-STILL ALIVE...
TH-THE MORTARS WAITED... UNTIL THE LINES FORMED...
WE MUST HELP THE WOUNDED ...UNTIL THE AMBULANCE COMES.
8

April 19, 1992

Dear Joe,

We're just listening on the news that the city of Mostar (we have been there, Joe, remember the old bridge?) is being destroyed by the Federal Army.

The army general Perisic made an ultimatum to the people of Mostar to return his two missing pilots until 6.00 P.M. otherwise he will destroy the whole city. The pilots were't returned, because nobody knows where they are. So, at 6.05 P.M. the army's artillery and the fighter planes started destroying the city (it is 7.30 P.M. at the moment). By the morning the whole city will be probably wiped out from the earth.

Love, Ervin

THAT NIGHT...
ERVIN...
EDVIN WOKE WITH A FEVER. HE'S BURNING UP.
DID YOU GIVE HIM AN ASPIRIN? AN ALCOHOL BATH-?

I'VE TRIED...WITH WHATEVER WE HAVE. NOTHING HELPS. WH-WHAT CAN WE DO?
WRAP HIM IN A BLANKET, EDINA.

I'LL TAKE HIM TO THE HOSPITAL. YOU STAY HERE WITH MAJA, EDINA.

P-PAPA... I DON'T FEEL... SO GOOD.
DON'T WORRY, EDVIN. YOU'LL BE ALL RIGHT.

JUST LIE BACK... REST, EDVIN. WE ARE ONLY MINUTES FROM THE HOSPITAL.
WE WILL BE THERE SOON. THEY WILL-
SA·244·196

SERB MILITIA!
10

OUT OF THE CAR! APPROACH SLOWLY WITH IDENTIFICATION PAPERS OUT.
IT IS NOT PERMITTED TO DRIVE AT NIGHT.
PLEASE.. LET ME EXPLAIN.
IT IS MY SON... HE IS TERRIBLY SICK. A FEVER. I MUST GET HIM TO HOSPITAL.

PFAH! A WASTE OF TIME. HE WILL NEVER SURVIVE. NO MATTER... GO AHEAD.

AS DAWN STREAKS LIGHT ACROSS THE HORIZON...
THE HOSPITAL ...AT LAST.

DOCTOR..PLEASE ..IT'S MY SON. HE HAS A TERRIBLE FEVER...
BRING HIM HERE.

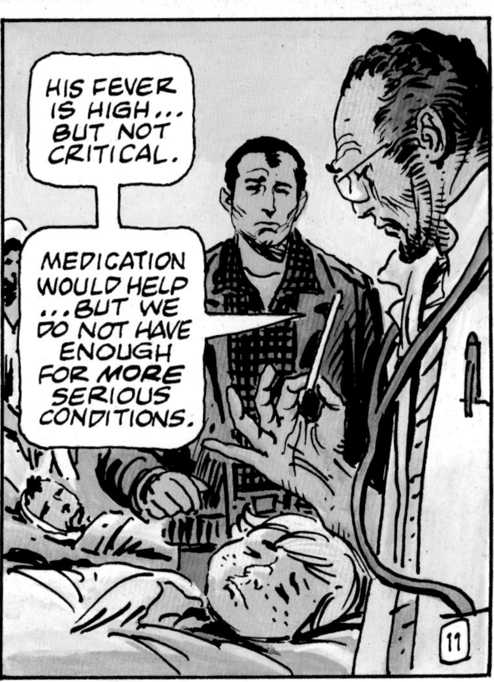
HIS FEVER IS HIGH... BUT NOT CRITICAL.
MEDICATION WOULD HELP ...BUT WE DO NOT HAVE ENOUGH FOR MORE SERIOUS CONDITIONS.
11

April 19, 1992

Dear Muriel,

I got the article you sent yesterday after midnight, thus that it was too late to forward it to anyone.

The last night was terrible for us. The Serbs were bombing the city the whole night and Edvin was having a terrible fever with a very high temperature. We couldn't take him to the doctor due to the police-hour, and were trying to lower the temperature using some old fashioned methods.

This morning we took him to the hospital which is only two miles far from us and were stopped by the Serbian militia four times. They all have searched us and the car and didn't care that the child is ill and has to see the doctor. The doctor said that he needs to receive six injections (penicillin), but that they don't have any. We're trying now to get those injections through some friends.

Can you only imagine how many poor people have sick ones and hungry ones in this war and can't do anything about it?

We're very much dissapointed with Cyrus Vance's mission here. He spent only a few hours in Sarajevo, and many more hours in Belgrade, where the Serbs told him only lies. He doesn't seem to be accusing Serbia very much for what's happening in Bosnia, although it is very clear to everyone in the world that they are doing all this. He also said that the U.N. troops will not come to Bosnia because there is no money. Also he doesn't agree with the sanctions and economic measures which the United States are intending to take against Serbia. He is trying to soften them now.

Love,

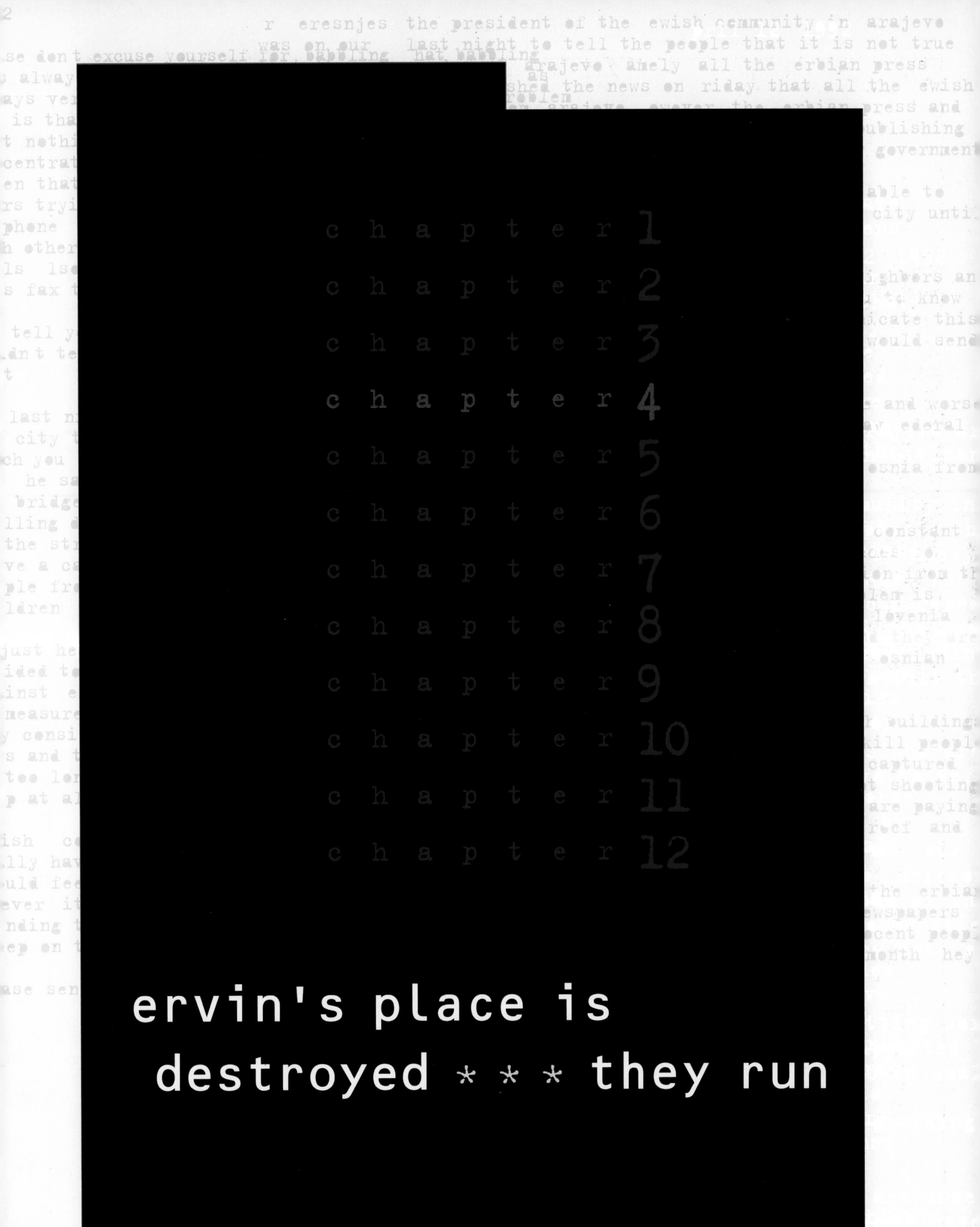
chapter 1
chapter 2
chapter 3
chapter 4
chapter 5
chapter 6
chapter 7
chapter 8
chapter 9
chapter 10
chapter 11
chapter 12
ervin's place is destroyed * * * they run

APRIL 1992... THE SITUATION IN SARAJEVO GROWS WORSE. ONCE-CARED-FOR PETS ROAM THE RUINED STREETS... SURVIVING SCAVENGERS.

AN ODD MIX OF PEDIGREES AND MUTTS... ABANDONED GROUPS OF PERSISTENT HUNTERS.

NOW THEY SEARCH FOR SCRAPS OF FOOD... TO STAY ALIVE. PITIFUL INDIVIDUALLY... DANGEROUS COLLECTIVELY.

LIKE THE OTHER INHABITANTS OF SARAJEVO, THEY HAVE BECOME VICTIMS OF WAR...

...UNABLE TO COMPREHEND WHY THEY MUST SUFFER... WHY NO ONE COMES TO THEIR AID.

THE SAME QUESTIONS FRUSTRATE AND CONFOUND THEIR HUMAN COUNTER-PARTS.

19/04 '92 16:25 ☎078 146072 HOLLAND 01

DEAR MURIEL & JOE

I CAN'T SAY I'M OPTIMISTIC ANYMORE. I JUST SAW A SNIPPET ON CNN, BUT BEFORE MY ATTENTION WAS FOCUSED (YOU KNOW HOW IT IS) SOME NAMES HAD ESCAPED ME. BUT THE GIST OF IT WAS THAT THE PEACE-KEEPING FORCE MIGHT BE WITHDRAWN FROM BOSNIA BECAUSE OF THE ONGOING FIGHTING. I JUST DON'T DARE TELL THIS TO ERVIN. I KEEP HOPING I MISUNDERSTOOD. ANYWAY, FOR YOU IT'S PASSOVER SEDER. FOR US, IT'S EASTER. LET'S PRAY FOR THE SAME THING. BEST WISHES. MARTIN

Strip Art Features, G. Dimitrova 49, 71000 Sarajevo, Bosnia-Herzegovina
Tel. (38-71) 455-225, 544-037, Telex 41539 saf yu, Fax (38-71) 46 43 41

April 20, 1992

Dear Muriel and Joe,

The U.S. ambassador in Belgrade Warren Zimmerman contacted the Federal Army head-quarters in Belgrade yesterday and succeeded to stop the bombing of Mostar at 7.30 P.M. It seems that he has a very strong position and a lot of powerful arguments, because such an action was not possible last year when the army was destroying Dubrovnik, Vukovar and other cities.

Unfortunately, a big part of Mostar was destroyed for those 90 minutes of constant bombing. Many houses and apartment buildings were in the fire the whole night because the army didn't allow the city's firemen to get to most of the places.

Edvin feels a bit better this morning after he received the second shot of penicillin. So, we hope for the best. It must be that he became ill after sleeping in the basement for several nights.

Love,

Ervin

2

A CRAZY WORLD INDEED. IT IS AS IF SARAJEVO EXISTS ON ANOTHER PLANET... BENT ON ITS OWN EXTERMINATION.
IN THE TOWN OF DOBRINJA ...A FEW MILES FROM SARAJEVO..
EDVIN. HOW ARE YOU FEELING?
BETTER, PAPA. COUGH, COUGH
YOU BETTER STOP SMOKING THOSE STRONG CIGARETTES, EDVIN... THEY'RE MAKING YOU COUGH!
I DON'T SMOKE, BUTZO. YOU-
OH... YOU'RE JUST JOKING ME.

WHREEEEEEEEEEEEE
KRUMPF
THOSE EXPLOSIONS ARE CLOSE, ERVIN. THE WHOLE HOUSE IS SHAKING...
EDINA.. YOU AND THE CHILDREN STAY DOWN HERE... IN THE STUDIO.
I'M GOING TO CHECK OUT-SIDE.
SKREEEEEEEEEEEEEE
I'LL GO WITH YOU, ERVIN.
3

THOSE BOMBS WERE CLOSE, ERVIN...BUT, NO CIGAR.
NOT THIS TIME, BUTZO-
ERVIN...I-I NEED SOME HELP. PLEASE.

WHAT IS IT, MIRKO?
ONE OF THE SHELLS TORE A RAFTER! IT'S MY FATHER-

HE'S TRAPPED IN HIS ROOM UPSTAIRS. WE CAN'T GET HIM OUT-
OF COURSE. COME ON, BUTZO... MIRKO'S HOUSE IS JUST NEXT DOOR.

STAY CALM, PAPA...WE'LL GET YOU OUT.
GRAB IT, BUTZO... AND LIFT!
DON'T WORRY, GRANDPA... WE'LL SAVE YOU.

AH, MIRKO. GLAD TO SEE YOU...
PAPA...
ARE YOU ALL RIGHT? Y-YOU'RE BLEEDING.
I'M FINE. RESTING. ... A BIT DUSTY.
WHAT'S THAT RUMBLING SOUND? IS IT THUNDER...?
IT'S... COMING CLOSER!
4

BLOM
WHUMP
19826

A TANK! HEADING THIS WAY!
KNOCKING DOWN EVERY HOUSE!

MIRKO... GATHER YOUR FAMILY. YOU MUST RUN!
RUN? WH-WHERE?

ANY-WHERE! I-I MUST GET BACK TO EDINA AND THE KIDS.

I'M GOING BACK TO MY HOME, ERVIN...
BE CAREFUL, BUTZO. STAY CLOSE TO THE HOUSES. GOOD LUCK.

I MUST GET BACK TO EDINA AND THE CHILDREN... BEFORE THE TANK REACHES OUR HOUSE...
KRUMP

ERVIN... THANK HEAVENS YOU'RE BACK! WHAT-
NO TIME, EDINA. WE HAVE TO GET OUT OF THE HOUSE...
5

THEY'RE SHELLING THE HOUSE..
ERVIN... WE MUST RUN! OUR- OUR THINGS...
WH-WHAT SHOULD WE TAKE? HOW-
M-MAMA.. THE HOUSE IS... SHAKING?

EDINA--THE LIST OF FAX NUMBERS...
M-MY ARTISTS' WORK... THE ORIGINALS. MY EQUIPMENT-
BRUMMP

PAPA... I AM SCARED..
DON'T WORRY, EDVIN... WE'LL BE-

KRUMPF

EDINA... HOLD MAJA'S HAND! STAY CLOSE TO ME!
WE'VE GOT TO GO!
THE PLACE IS ON FIRE!
6

RUN, EDINA.. RUN!

D-DON'T GASP LOOK...BACK- GASP

KEEP... GASP RUNNING!

METHODICALLY, THE TANK PROCEEDS TO DEMOLISH EVERY HOUSE IN THE AREA.
BLAMPF
WHRUMP
WHUMP
APPARENTLY, THEIR MISSION IS TO MAKE CERTAIN THAT NOT ONE BRICK REMAINS ATOP ANOTHER.

IN THE FIELD BEHIND THE FURNACE OF DESTROYED HOMES...
ERVIN... IT IS OUR NEIGHBORS.
MIRKO... ZVONKO.

ERVIN--YOU'RE ALIVE! YOU MADE IT... WITH YOUR FAMILY...
WE THOUGHT THEY KILLED YOU.

WE MUST FIND ANOTHER PLACE... FOR SAFETY... BEFORE THEY CATCH US IN THE OPEN. GASP
7

ERVIN... I- I CAN'T... GASP
PLEASE, EDINA GASP WE... MUST... KEEP GOING GASP

I... CAN'T! MY HEART GASP-GASP IS TEARING OUT... OF GASP MY CHEST-
THAT BUILDING. W-WE... WILL REST THERE ... EDINA...

IT IS ICKY, PAPA... WET AND MUDDY.
I KNOW, EDVIN. BUT... WE CANNOT GO FARTHER. WE MUST STAY HERE.. FOR TONIGHT.
STAY IN THE CORNER BY THE WALL.

ALL THROUGH THE NIGHT THE BOMBARDMENT CONTINUES WITH UNCEASING INTENSITY...
KRUMPF
WHUMP
GRUMMP
WHREEEEEEEEEE
WHUMP
WHUMP

SLEEP IS ELUSIVE. COLD, FEAR, AND IMMINENT DEATH ARE CONSTANT COMPANIONS.
8

20/06/1992 FROM STRIP ART FEATURES TO KUBERT P.01

April 21, 1992

Dear Muriel and Joe,

We're still alive, although there is enormous shooting very close to this area. The city's defenders are calling everybody who has a gun or weapon to protect their houses against Serbian terrorists.

People are very much frightened, because the Serbian's specialty is to come into people's homes, kill and steal all valuable things.

They just said on the radio that the Serbs didn't succeed in taking over the TV station and TV studios and that the defenders are still holding tight. It would be a disaster if the Serbs take over our TV, which is the most objective one that ever existed in this part of the world. In Serbia, TV and the press are the servants of Milosevic and his regime.

I'm sending you the fax which I received from Jacques Post from Holland today.

Love, Ervin

Dear Ervin,

Diplomatic movements seem to be escalating. Front page AD today: 'USA and EC are threatenting to break off all diplomatic traffic with Belgrade as protest against the Serbian violence in the republic Bosnia-Hercegowina. The USA and the countries of the EC are considering to withdraw their diplomats from Belgrade. The American department of Foreign Affairs gave out a press release saying that there are talks "at the highest level" to decide what actions must be taken.' The USA and EC are having a get together today. They are exceptionally angry because the Serbs wear 'blue helmets'! UN cars and jeeps are stolen and used the by the Serbs.

AD journalist, Michel Thomassen, was in Foca this weekend and wrote an article today that he had met six different groups of Serbs, operating independently. One of the soldiers is quoted, saying: 'The UN and the EC has set this up, this civilian war, and now it is our problem. Just look around real good. Here the Third World War will start. All these so called Serbian freedom fighters give me the impression that the war, to them, is great fun.'

Last news on the radio: various European politicians said today that they're 'outraged' by what is happening in your country. Milosevic, however, had said that all this is 'beyond him'. One thing is for sure, the asshole can never win this, which, at the same time, is the bad thing about it. As soon as I'll know more, I'll let you know.

Love to all of you – Jacques

CAUTIOUSLY, THE FAMILY STEPS INTO THE DUST-ENCRUSTED LANDSCAPE OF A BESIEGED DOBRINJA...
THE TANK IS GONE, ERVIN.
PERHAPS...FOR NOW, EDINA...
...BUT...WE HAVEN'T SEEN THE LAST OF THEM. THAT IS CERTAIN!

THE ONLY THINGS I WAS ABLE TO SAVE FROM OUR HOME... SOME MONEY... MY WATCH...

...AND THIS SLIGHTLY MELTED "YELLOW KID" STATUETTE. AN AWARD. FROM LUCCA. FOR MY PUBLICATIONS.

NOW-- ALL YOUR WORK IS GONE, ERVIN. OH, MY DEAR-
EDINA...AS LONG AS WE ARE TOGETHER.. AND GET THROUGH THIS HELL.. THAT IS THE MOST IMPORTANT THING.

Holiday Inn HOTELS
WE MUST HEAD FOR THE CITY. IF THE HOLIDAY INN HOTEL IS STILL INTACT... I KNOW THE MANAGER.
ALSO- THEY MAY HAVE A FAX MACHINE.

SOON WE WILL HAVE FOOD... TELEPHONE.. A PLACE TO REST.
BUT...WE MUST BE CAREFUL. SNIPERS ARE EVERYWHERE.
10

IT'S SO STRANGE, ERVIN. JUST A FEW MONTHS AGO, DOBRINJA WAS CALM... PEACEFUL... A SWEET NEIGHBORHOOD.
NOW... IT'S LIKE A CEMETERY!

I HOPE BUTZO GOT HOME ALL RIGHT.
I AM ASHAMED TO SAY I HAVEN'T EVEN THOUGHT OF BUTZO, ERVIN.

I ONCE HAD AN ASSISTANT ..NAME OF SENAD..LIVED IN THIS AREA.
DO YOU REMEMBER THE ADDRESS?

IT LOOKS BADLY DAMAGED, ERVIN.
I THINK IT'S NEAR HERE. YES... YES! JUST ACROSS THE STREET. THAT'S THE HOUSE.

THIS PLACE... HAS A SMELL OF DEATH. LIKE A TOMB.
11

NEW YORK TIMES *JUNE 21, 1992*

Serbs Seize More Towns

GORAZDE, Bosnia and Herzegovina, April 20 (AP) — Thousands of refugees trekked through forests or crammed into vehicles today to flee advancing Serbian forces seeking control over a swath of Bosnia and Herzegovina.

Serbian forces have overrun Bratunac and Srebrenica, Muslim-dominated towns along the Serbian border, since Sunday after capturing about half a dozen others in previous weeks, news reports said.

DEAR ERVIN —

WE DON'T KNOW WHAT TO SAY. YOUR LETTER SEEMS FROM ANOTHER WORLD. WE CAN ONLY IMAGINE WHAT YOU ARE ALL GOING THROUGH. WE ALL HOPE AND PRAY IT WILL BE OVER SOON.

WE'RE SENDING COPIES OF YOUR LETTER TO THE PEOPLE WE KNOW -- TO TRY TO GET IT INTO THE N.Y. TIMES. WE'RE ALSO CONTACTING OUR JERSEY NEWSPAPERS -- TO TRY AND GET IT PRINTED - SO EVERYONE CAN LEARN OF THE TERRIBLE THINGS GOING ON IN SARAJEVO -- AND, MAYBE GET SOMETHING MOVING HERE.

TAKE CARE OF YOURSELVES -- STAY LOW -- IT CAN'T LAST FOREVER.

LOVE FROM US ALL TO ALL OF YOU —
JOE & MURIEL

c h a p t e r 1

c h a p t e r 2

c h a p t e r 3

c h a p t e r 4

c h a p t e r 5

c h a p t e r 6

c h a p t e r 7

c h a p t e r 8

c h a p t e r 9

c h a p t e r 10

c h a p t e r 11

c h a p t e r 12

the run to sarajevo

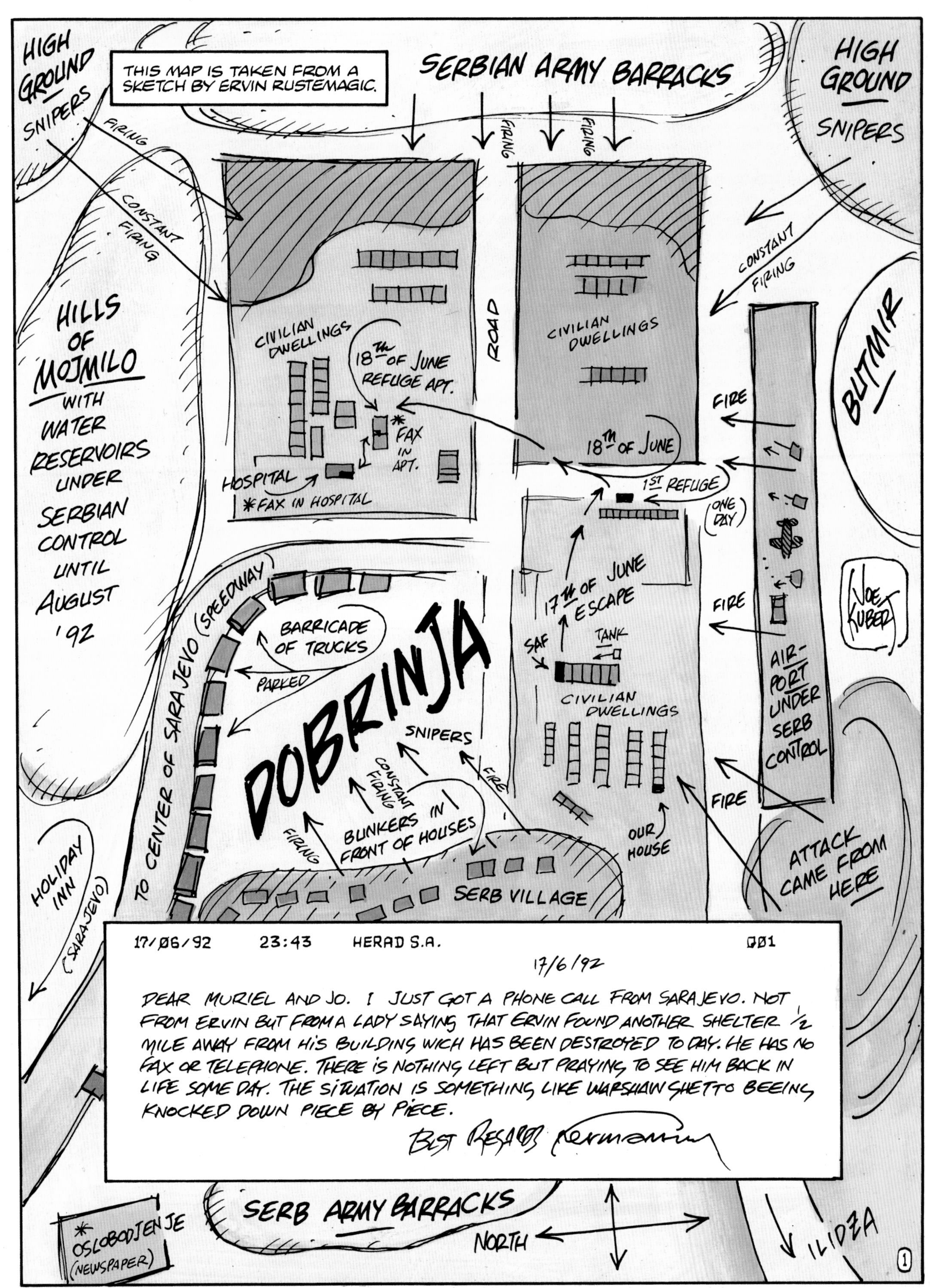
HIGH GROUND
SNIPERS
THIS MAP IS TAKEN FROM A SKETCH BY ERVIN RUSTEMAGIC.
SERBIAN ARMY BARRACKS
HIGH GROUND
SNIPERS
FIRING
FIRING
FIRING
CONSTANT FIRING
CONSTANT FIRING
HILLS OF MOJMILO WITH WATER RESERVOIRS UNDER SERBIAN CONTROL UNTIL AUGUST '92
CIVILIAN DWELLINGS
18TH OF JUNE REFUGE APT.
* FAX IN APT.
HOSPITAL
* FAX IN HOSPITAL
ROAD
CIVILIAN DWELLINGS
18TH OF JUNE
1ST REFUGE
ONE DAY
BUTMIR
FIRE
FIRE
FIRE
17TH OF JUNE ESCAPE
SAF
TANK
CIVILIAN DWELLINGS
AIRPORT UNDER SERB CONTROL
BARRICADE OF TRUCKS
PARKED
TO CENTER OF SARAJEVO (SPEEDWAY)
DOBRINJA
SNIPERS
CONSTANT FIRING
FIRE
FIRING
BUNKERS IN FRONT OF HOUSES
OUR HOUSE
SERB VILLAGE
ATTACK CAME FROM HERE
HOLIDAY INN (SARAJEVO)
JOE KUBERT
17/06/92 23:43 HERAD S.A. 001
17/6/92
DEAR MURIEL AND JO. I JUST GOT A PHONE CALL FROM SARAJEVO. NOT FROM ERVIN BUT FROM A LADY SAYING THAT ERVIN FOUND ANOTHER SHELTER 1/2 MILE AWAY FROM HIS BUILDING WICH HAS BEEN DESTROYED TO DAY. HE HAS NO FAX OR TELEPHONE. THERE IS NOTHING LEFT BUT PRAYING TO SEE HIM BACK IN LIFE SOME DAY. THE SITUATION IS SOMETHING LIKE WARSHAW GHETTO BEEING KNOCKED DOWN PIECE BY PIECE.
BEST REGARDS
SERB ARMY BARRACKS
* OSLOBODJENJE (NEWSPAPER)
NORTH
ILIDZA
1

IN THE SUBURB OF DOBRINJA IN SARAJEVO, THE SHELLING AND SNIPER FIRE IS UNCEASING...
KEEP DOWN, EDINA.. KEEP EDVIN CLOSE.
NO ONE KNOWS WHERE THE NEXT GRENADE WILL LAND OR WHO WILL BE STRUCK BY THE NEXT BULLET.

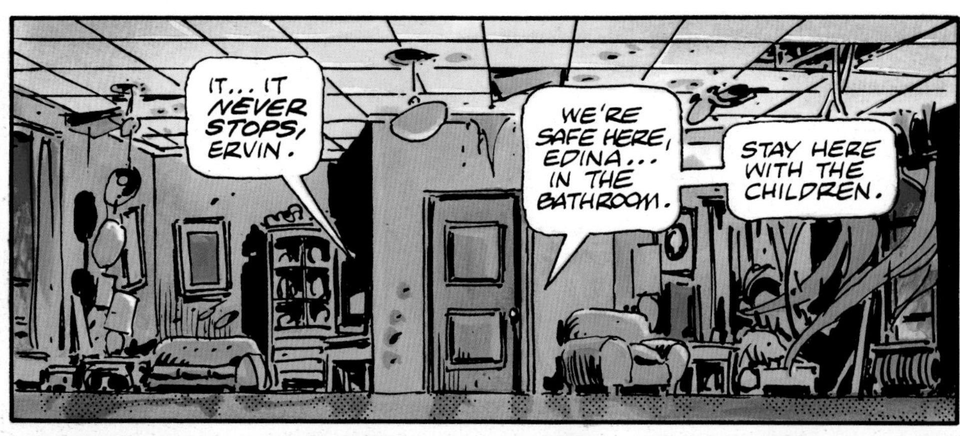
IT... IT NEVER STOPS, ERVIN.
WE'RE SAFE HERE, EDINA... IN THE BATHROOM.
STAY HERE WITH THE CHILDREN.

WHY? WHERE ARE YOU GOING?
I MUST GET THE CAR...
DON'T GO, PAPA-

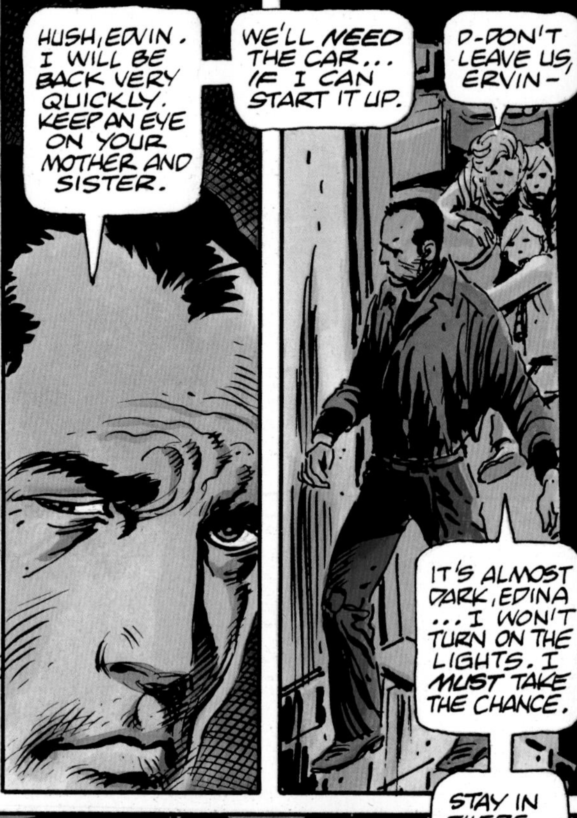
HUSH, EDVIN. I WILL BE BACK VERY QUICKLY. KEEP AN EYE ON YOUR MOTHER AND SISTER.
WE'LL NEED THE CAR... IF I CAN START IT UP.
D-DON'T LEAVE US, ERVIN-
IT'S ALMOST DARK, EDINA ... I WON'T TURN ON THE LIGHTS. I MUST TAKE THE CHANCE.
STAY IN THERE... WITH THE KIDS.

STRANGE... HOW WE HUMANS CAN GROW ACCUSTOMED TO THE MOST TERRIBLE THINGS.
AT FIRST THE SHELLING SCARED ME SO ...I COULDN'T EVEN MOVE. NOW... I CAN HARDLY HEAR IT...

KRUMPF
...ALMOST HARDLY.
2

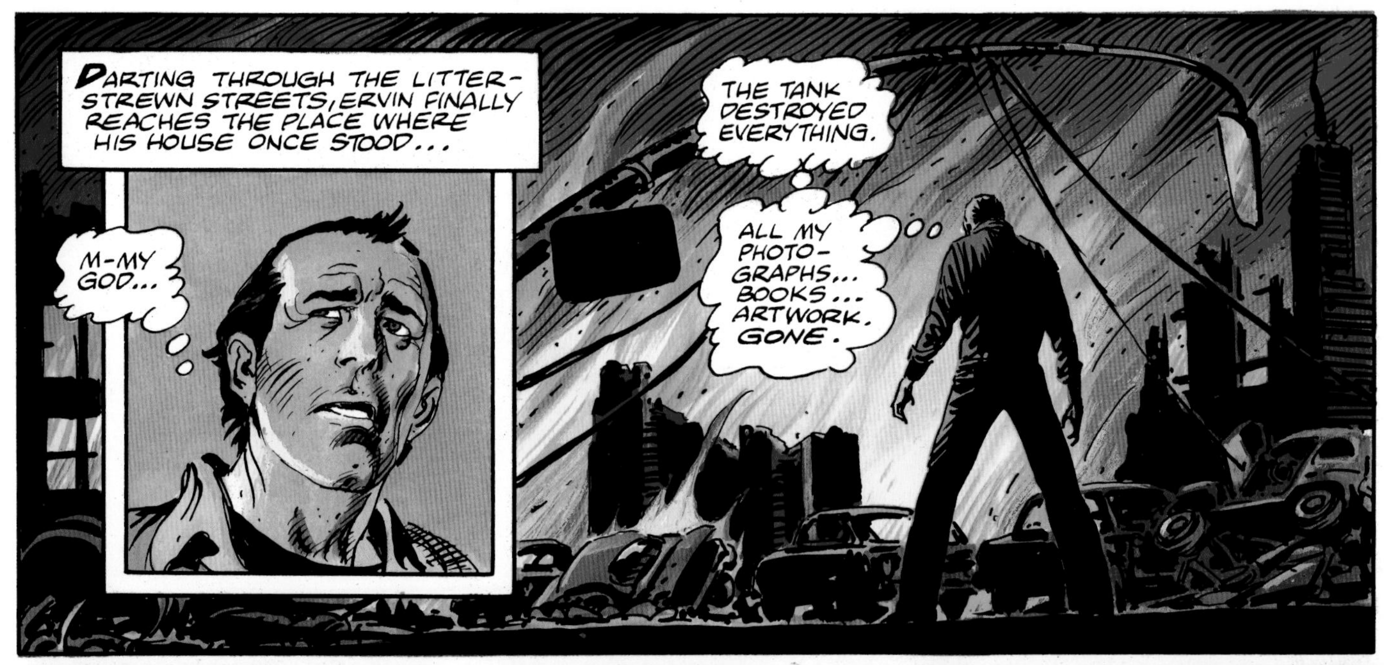
DARTING THROUGH THE LITTER-STREWN STREETS, ERVIN FINALLY REACHES THE PLACE WHERE HIS HOUSE ONCE STOOD...
M-MY GOD...
THE TANK DESTROYED EVERYTHING.
ALL MY PHOTO-GRAPHS... BOOKS... ARTWORK. GONE.

HERE IT IS... MY LITTLE OPEL KADET.
NOW... WILL IT START?

KLIK-THRUMM

AHH... THANK YOU, GOD.

SEVERAL VEHICLES AHEAD A TERRIFIC EXPLOSION RIPS THE AIR... FOLLOWED BY A PIERCING SCREAM OF PAIN.
A WILD SHELL.
ERVIN HYPER-VENTILATES... IT IS DIFFICULT TO BREATHE.
S-SOMEONE ...CAUGHT IT.
3

SOMEONE WAS HIT! ARE THEY ALIVE?
I - I MUST TRY... TO HELP...

UNH...

IT... HURTS. D-DON'T LEAVE ME...
I'M HERE. I'LL HELP YOU.
HE'S BADLY TORN UP. THE WOUNDS ARE VERY DEEP...

HOLD ON. I'M WITH YOU... I WILL NOT LEAVE YOU.
JUST A SHORT WAY TO MY CAR... HOLD ON.

HOLD ON ... THE HOSPITAL IS ONLY A FEW BLOCKS FROM HERE.

EASY... THAT'S IT. THE DOCTORS INSIDE WILL TAKE CARE OF YOU.
OHH..

THIS WAS ONCE A SUPERMARKET. NOW... IT'S AN EMERGENCY HOSPITAL. IT SEEMS PRIORITIES HAVE CHANGED FOR US BOSNIANS.

I-I NEED HELP. THIS MAN NEEDS A DOCTOR-
IT IS GOOD THAT YOU GOT HIM HERE SO FAST. OTHERS ARE NOT SO LUCKY. WE HAVE FEW AMBULANCES...
MY CAR STILL WORKS.
THIS WAY. BRING HIM IN HERE.
NURSE! SUTURES.. SALINE.

HERE IS THE KEY TO MY CAR, DOCTOR. YOU HAVE JUST ACQUIRED A NEW AMBULANCE.

THANK YOU. BUT--HOW WILL YOU GET BACK HOME?
I AM LESS THAN A MILE AWAY. I'LL BE ALL RIGHT.
GOOD-BYE.

IT'S ALMOST DAWN... BUT... THE SKY IS STILL BLACK WITH SMOKE. THE BOMB BLASTS NEVER STOP.

EDINA... WHAT HAPPENED?
ARE YOU HURT? THE CHILDREN-
5
PAPA... PAPA...

NO, NO... YOUR WIFE IS NOT HURT. IT... IS HER NERVES.
THE BOMBS... THE SHOOTING. IT AFFECTS EVERY-ONE.
M-MAMA IS CRYING, PAPA...

ERVIN... I'M FRIGHTENED. =SOB= THE BOMBS. THEY NEVER STOP. CHILDREN... PEOPLE-- DYING IN THE STREETS =SOB= IN... THEIR HOMES...

I'M FRIGHTENED FOR YOU... FOR EDVIN... MAJA.. =SOB=
OH, MY DEAR.
THERE IS A BOMB SHELTER IN THIS BUILDING. MANY OF THE TENANTS FEEL MORE SAFE DOWN THERE. LESS NOISE. THEY CAN SLEEP.

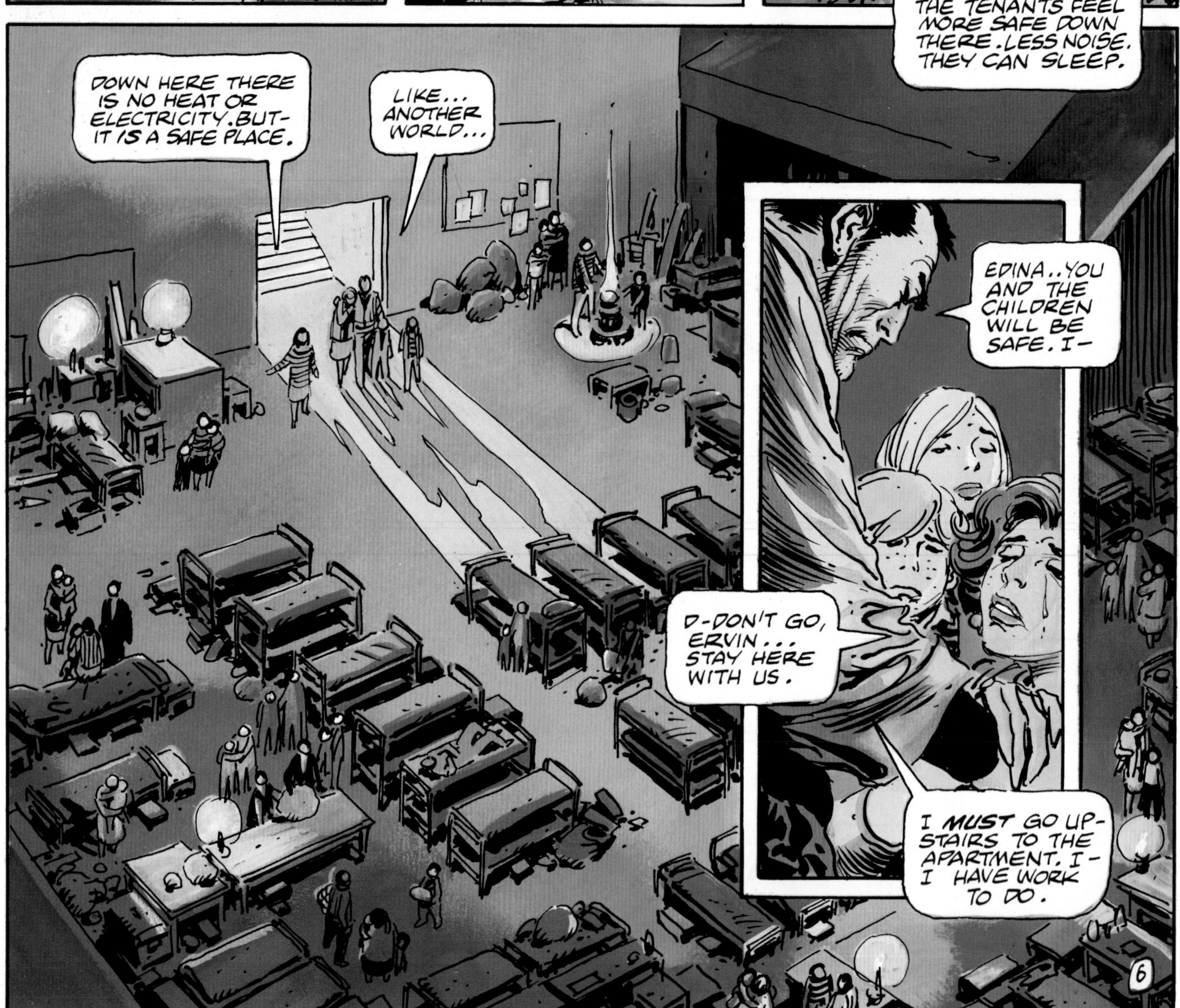
DOWN HERE THERE IS NO HEAT OR ELECTRICITY. BUT IT IS A SAFE PLACE.
LIKE... ANOTHER WORLD...
EDINA.. YOU AND THE CHILDREN WILL BE SAFE. I-
D-DON'T GO, ERVIN... STAY HERE WITH US.
I MUST GO UP-STAIRS TO THE APARTMENT. I-I HAVE WORK TO DO.
6

SARAJEVO, JUNE 18, 1992 - 22h46

DEAR MYRIEL & JOE

YESTERDAY, AT 6.30 A.M. A HEAVY ATTACK ON OUR AREA STARTED. SEVERAL TANKS AND TRANSPORTERS CAME IN OUR STREETS AND STARTED DESTROYING EVERYTHING THERE. ONE TANK CAME IN FRONT OF THE BUILDING WHERE EVERYTHING FELL APPART AFTER SEVERAL GRENADES. OUR HOUSE IS ALSO DESTROYED. WE HAVE NOTHING ANY MORE. HOWEVER, WE SUCCEEDED TO ESCAPE WITH SOME NEIGHBOURS ONE MILE AWAY AND WE ARE STAYING WITH SOME FRIENDS HERE. UNFORTUNATELY, WE DIDN'T HAVE TIME TO BRING ANYTHING WITH US AT ALL, AS WE HAD TO CARRY OUR CHILDREN, WHILE WE WERE RUNNING AWAY.

SERBS HAVE KILLED HUNDREDS OF CIVILIANS IN OUR RESIDENTIAL AREA YESTERDAY AND TODAY. THE SITUATION IS MUCH WORSE THAN THE WORST HELL.

I'LL TRY TO FAX THIS THROUGH. PLEASE FORWARD THIS TO THE OTHERS. TRY TO FAX ME A.S.A.P., BECAUSE WE CAN RUN OUT OF ELECTRICITY.

PLEASE ALSO FORWARD THIS TO HERMANN AND TO MARTIN AND JACQUES.

LOVE,
ERVIN

7

JULI08, 1992 13:40 "MILLS" SARAJEVO OML. BRIGADA 9 FAX:38 71 450 148 02

Sarajevo, July 8, 1992

Dear Joe,

This is Wednesday morning, and we're still alive, but I am afraid not for very long. We lost our house, our offices, my mother's house, cars and everything else that we were earning, buying and collecting in the past twenty years . . . But, worst of all, we lost all our hopes that we will survive this horror and that we will be ever able to get away from this hell.

Everything that the world is doing, all those political discussions and nonsenses are only giving more time and more opportunities to the Serbian fascist leader Milosevic to kill and destroy. And Serbs are increasing shelling and bombing every day. So, all we are getting are grenades, bullets and some mineral water, which represent most of the humanitarian aid that comes from France.

I have no more words to explain how we live and what we feel. Our children, who are suffering for 95 days now, closed between the walls, are getting out of their minds. Edina can't stop crying, and I have no arguments to calm them down and tell them that the things will get better, because they're not going better. They are going worse and worse every day, and it seems to be an interest of civilized world not to stop this human tragedy. And I am sure that Bosnia-Herzegovina will be the biggest human tragedy and catastrophe in the history of civilization. There are about 200.000 people killed and massacred so far, over 150.000 are in Serbian concentration camps, prepared for execution, over one million people had to escape from their homes, etc. . . And world, who knows all that, is just sitting, watching, discussing and finding hundreds of reasons for not doing anything.

To all of us here it looks ridiculous now when we look back and remember some terrorists' actions in Italy, France or England . . . When terrorists have killed 5, 6 or dozen persons. How much fuss was made about such terrorists' acts ?!? And we have here hundreds of such terrorists' acts every day and nobody cares! New York, London, Paris, Rome or Hamburg are being very much shocked when a bomb explodes in metro or railway station . . . And only in our district of Dobrinja (residential area of Sarajevo where we live) over 250.000 bombs and grenades have exploded so far . . .

Lots of love to everyone,

Ervin

A TRICKLE OF GREY SMOKE RISES FROM THE EIGHTH FLOOR OF A POCK-MARKED BUILDING IN DOBRINJA... INTO THE MORNING AIR.
THIS IS AWFUL, ERVIN...
DON'T BURN THE POTATOES, MAMA...
MY EYES ARE TEARING SO I CAN'T EVEN SEE THEM, MAJA.
YOU'RE DOING FINE, EDINA-
WAIT. SOMEONE IS AT THE DOOR. MAYBE A NEIGHBOR COMPLAINING... ABOUT YOUR COOKING?
KNOCK KNOCK
HELLO. WHO'S TRYING TO BURN DOWN THE BUILDING?
BRANKO! WHERE DID YOU COME FROM? I HEARD YOU WERE IN SARAJEVO?
HOW DID YOU FIND US?
NOT DIFFICULT, ERVIN. I JUST FOLLOWED THE SMELL OF EDINA'S =SNIFF= CUISINE.

SERIOUSLY, I COME WITH A MESSAGE FOR YOU. FROM THE MINISTRY IN SARAJEVO. THERE IS A CHANCE THAT YOU AND YOUR FAMILY CAN GET OUT.

YOUR FRIENDS IN FRANCE AND BELGIUM AND THE UNITED STATES HAVE MADE CONTACT WITH GOVERNMENT PEOPLE.
BUT...YOU MUST BE AVAILABLE TO LEAVE AT A MOMENT'S NOTICE.
I REALIZE... I MUST GO.
YOU MUST GET INTO SARAJEVO. TO THE MINISTRY... NOW!
W-WOULD YOU LIKE SOME SOUP, BRANKO?
9

THAT NIGHT..
I UNDERSTAND, ERVIN... AND, OF COURSE YOU MAY USE THE OPEL. AFTER ALL, IT IS YOURS.
THANK YOU, DOCTOR. I WILL RETURN THE CAR... UNLESS...
IT IS DANGEROUS. BUT... IT IS A TRIP WE MUST MAKE OFTEN.
THIS HOSPITAL IS NOT EQUIPPED TO TAKE CARE OF SERIOUS OR CRITICAL WOUNDS...
...SO... PATIENTS MUST BE TAKEN TO THE HOSPITAL IN SARAJEVO. A TRIP LESS THAN TEN MILES. BUT... IT IS LIKE RUNNING A GAUNTLET.
HILLS OF MOJMILO
ROAD
SNIPERS FIRE
TRUCKS
TO SARAJEVO
THE SERBS HAVE DOBRINJA UNDER SIEGE. ARTILLERY AND SNIPERS FIRE AT ANYONE TRYING TO LEAVE... LIVING TARGETS.
THE MOST DANGEROUS PART IS HERE... JUST OUTSIDE THE HOSPITAL... FOR ABOUT A MILE.
WE LINE UP TRUCKS ALONG THE ROAD... BETWEEN THE SERB GUNS AND OUR ROUTE.
TO SARAJEVO
TRUCKS

MY OLD OPEL LOOKS DIFFERENT, DOCTOR.
YES... WELL, THE SERBS USE THE RED CROSS AS A BULL'S EYE. SO WE PUT METAL PLATES ON THE CAR... TO DEFLECT BULLETS.
WHAT IS THIS? COMIC BOOKS?
DON'T LAUGH. THAT'S ADDITIONAL ARMOR. TWO OR THREE COPIES CAN STOP A BULLET OR A BOMB SPLINTER.
10

THE SERB GUNS ARE ON THE OUTSIDE OF THE ROAD. YOU MUST DRIVE CLOSE TO THE TRUCKS... AND AS FAST AS YOU CAN!
BE CAREFUL OF THE DITCH ON THE OTHER SIDE, ERVIN.
START OUT SLOWLY.. UNTIL YOU GET PAST THE FIRST TRUCK... THEN... PUSH THE GAS PEDAL THROUGH THE FLOOR BOARD! GOOD LUCK.
I'M PAST THE FIRST TRUCK.. THE POINT OF NO RETURN.
EDINA... EDVIN... MAJA...
TRANS
THIS IS ALL... A DREAM. THIS... ISN'T ME. I'M NOT HERE... THIS ISN'T HAPPENING. IT'S A DREAM.
11

JULI 17, 1992 14:11 "MILLS" SARAJEVO OML. BRIGADA 9 FAX:38 71 450 148 STR.

Sarajevo, 17th of July 1992

Dear Muriel and Joe,

Today is 17th of July. The situation in the meantime became only worse, and we have less and less hope that we will stay alive, in spite of what you, Joe, are saying.

If somebody was killing and massacring penguins the way Serbs are massacring Bosnian people, the world would have intervened and would have taken stronger and faster measures. However, in our case, everybody is just sitting, talking and watching how thousands of innocent civillians are being killed, how dozens of homes are being destroyed, how the whole new state, recognized by the entire world and U.N., is being brought to misery . . . and who cares ?!?

It is very difficult to explain and describe how we feel. Old people who survived the Second World War said that it was <u>nothing</u> compared to our catastrophe. Still, this is happenning in the middle of Europe and on the door-step of 21st century.

Maja will have her 10th birtday on July 20th, and the only thing she is wishing is that w e all stay alive.

Love,

Ervin

c h a p t e r 1

c h a p t e r 2

c h a p t e r 3

c h a p t e r 4

c h a p t e r 5

c h a p t e r 6

c h a p t e r 7

c h a p t e r 8

c h a p t e r 9

c h a p t e r 10

c h a p t e r 11

c h a p t e r 12

the birthday party

JULI 20, 1992   20:14   "MILLS" SARAJEVO OML. BRIGADA 9   FAX:38 71 450 148 STR.

Sarajevo, July 20th, 1992

Dear Joe,

Today is Maja's 10th birthday. Edina prepared a very modest celebration, under constant gun-fire and detonations of exploding grenades.

Still, we felt somehow happy . . . mostly because we all are still alive . . . And then, only one hour ago, I got the information that the serbs have burned down my office building and that nothing is left there . . .

All the originals, all the life memories, photographs and negatives of our children, everthing I was collecting and bringing there with very much care and very much love . . . E v e r y t h i n g is gone forever !!!

You, Joe, and Muriel, w ho were in my office, know very well how much all that did mean to me. How much I was proud of that original of "Prince Valiant" from 1956, dedicated to me by Foster, and all other 12.000 (twelve thousand) originals that I had there . . .

Edina can't stop crying and I am hiding my tears from her . . . More than one half of my life has been burned down, and a great part of hers. I was spending all my time in that office, and very seldom with her and the children.

Still, w e should be happy to be alive. But, for how long ? . . .

Love,
Ervin

JULY 20TH, '92/MONDAY

DEAR ERVIN, EDINA, MAJA & EDVIN—

IT IS A VERY DIFFICULT THING TO TRY TO "CELEBRATE" A YOUNG LADY'S 10TH BIRTHDAY UNDER SUCH TERRIBLE CONDITIONS. BUT YOU MUST ALL CONSOLE YOURSELVES BY THE FACT THAT MAJA'S NEXT BIRTHDAY WILL BE DIFFERENT.

I KNOW THAT NONE OF US OUTSIDE CAN EVEN IMAGINE THE HORRORS YOU ARE ALL EXPERIENCING--NEVERTHELESS, YOU MUST THINK OF A BETTER TOMORROW--NO MATTER HOW DIFFICULT IT IS. YOU HAVE NO OPTIONS--NO CHOICES! TO THINK OTHERWISE IS TO CAPITULATE TO THE BARBARIANS! AND THAT IS EXACTLY WHAT THEY WANT. THEN--THERE IS NO ACCOUNTABILITY AND NO JUSTICE. SO--THAT, YOU CANNOT DO.

THE OFFICE--THE ARTWORK--THE COLLECTIONS--IN COMPARISON TO YOU AND YOUR FAMILY, ERVIN, THEY ARE NOTHING! WHEN YOU AND YOUR FAMILY GET OUT, YOU'LL START WITH A FRESH, CLEAN SLATE. AND THE PAST WILL GIVE TREMENDOUS NON-STOPPABLE MOMENTUM TO THE FUTURE. AND THE FUTURE IS EVERYTHING!

YOU WILL SURVIVE--AND YOU WILL GET OUT. AND WHEN YOU DO, ALL YOUR FRIENDS WILL BE THERE TO GREET YOU. WHENEVER AND WHEREVER IT IS! HOLD TOGETHER, ERVIN--EACH DAY BRINGS YOU CLOSER TO THAT TIME. YOU MUST BELIEVE IT!

LOVE TO ALL—
JOE

1

MAD MAX HAS BECOME A REALITY. ERVIN JAMS DOWN ON THE GAS PEDAL OF THE OPEL... AND ROARS PAST THE BARRICADE OF RUSTING TRUCKS...
BEEEEEEOW
BWEEEEEE
ZIP
TZING
VUMP
UP
TOOMP
PATATA
THE STEEL PLATES DEFLECT THE SERB BULLETS... BUT... COMIC-BOOKS AS PROTECTION?
I HAVE BECOME A COMIC-BOOK CHARACTER. MAYBE... I AM SUPERMAN?
IF SO... I DON'T NEED ANY PROTECTION.
BRAKKATATATATATATATAT
MY GOD... I AM GOING CRAZY.
REPAC • S.ELMO

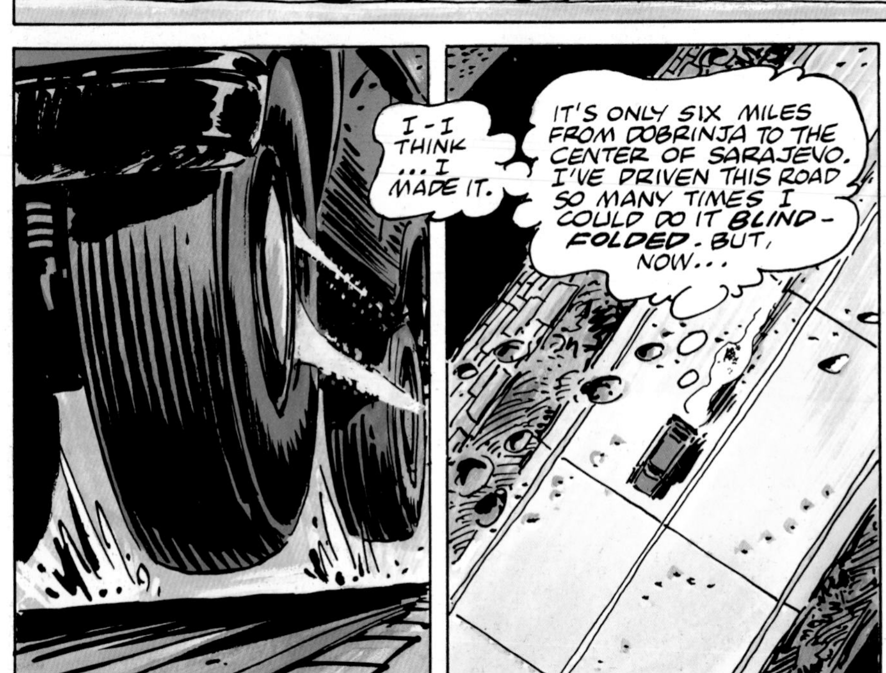
I - I THINK ... I MADE IT.
IT'S ONLY SIX MILES FROM DOBRINJA TO THE CENTER OF SARAJEVO. I'VE DRIVEN THIS ROAD SO MANY TIMES I COULD DO IT BLIND-FOLDED. BUT, NOW...

... IT IS ALIEN! THE LONGEST SIX MILES OF MY LIFE!
2

I DON'T THINK ONE BUILDING IN SARAJEVO IS LEFT UNDAMAGED.

NOT ONE WINDOW IS UNBROKEN.

SARAJEVO WAS CALLED "THE PEARL ON EARTH -- SNOW PEAKS KISSING THE SKY..."

WILL IT EVER AGAIN BE AS IT WAS?

I MUST FIND NIJAZ... IN THE MINISTRY BUILDING. HE IS AN OLD FRIEND.
ERVIN... SO. YOU ARE STILL ALIVE. THAT IS A GOOD BEGINNING.
IT IS GOOD TO SEE YOU, TOO, NIJAZ. YOU HAVE NEWS FOR ME?

SIT, ERVIN.
YOUR NAME HAS COME UP FROM MANY SOURCES. FAXES AND LETTERS FROM FRANCE... BELGIUM... SWITZERLAND... THE UNITED STATES.
YOU HAVE MANY FRIENDS.

THEY ALL WANT TO HELP YOU. AND... THERE IS A CHANCE THAT YOU AND YOUR FAMILY MAY BE EVACUATED.
BUT... THAT OPPORTUNITY MAY COME AT A MOMENT'S NOTICE. FOR THAT, YOU MUST BE IMMEDIATELY AVAILABLE.
EDINA AND THE CHILDREN ARE IN DOBRINJA. HOW-?
3

JULI 24, 1992 10:15 "MILLS" SARAJEVO OML. BRIGADA 9 FAX:38 71 450 148 STR.

July 22, 1992

Dear Andreas,

Two days ago (July 20) my daughter Maja had her 10th birthday. And, although we are the guests in this building with nothing of our own, and although there was a war going on with constant gun-fire and detonations of exploding grenades outside, my wife Edina has tried to prepare a very modest celebration. She made a cake of flour, sugar and pudding, as she didn't have eggs or anything else. Maja borrowed some clothes from a neighbour's girl and together with her 5-year old brother Edvin she decorated the room using some of the Christmas' tree decorations. A dozen of children, mostly refugees like we are, arrived around 4 P.M. The windows were shaking from the grenades that were exploding in the street, in front of the building, but children were smiling and playing in that room on the fourth floor, in which we put some furniture in front of the windows . . .

I was worried about photographs and negatives of our children Maja and Edvin, taken in the past ten years, on which we had all their birthdays, their grandparents, their friends, first school days, their holidays . . . I was worried about many other memories and other things that I was collecting with much love in the past 22 years, and bringing them from all over the world . . .

And all that disappeared in the fire set by Serbian killers and looters — miserable human beings.

I know that it is the most important thing to stay alive now. But it is hard to imagine that everything you have been building up in the past 22 years, is gone.

Love,

Ervin

6

HOURS RUN INTO DAYS... WEEKS INTO MONTHS... THE SNIPING AND THE SHELLING IN SARAJEVO GOES ON. AND... SOME SORT OF LIFE GOES ON.

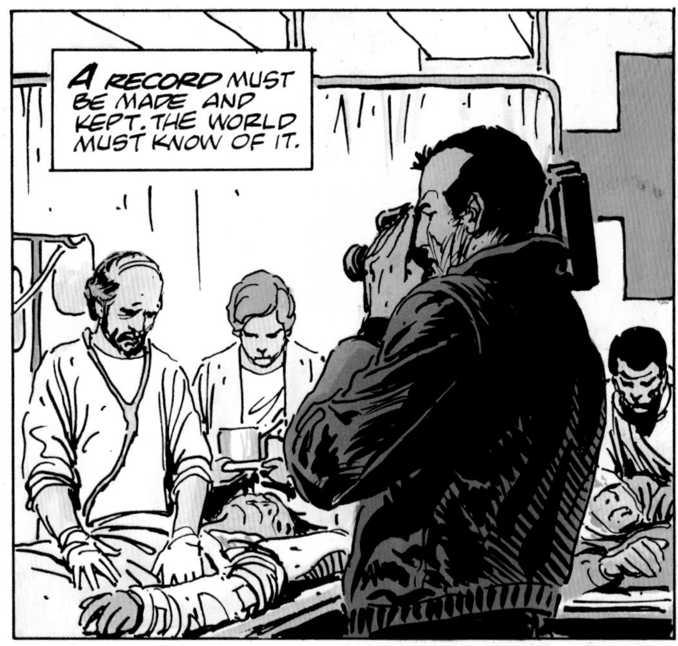
A RECORD MUST BE MADE AND KEPT. THE WORLD MUST KNOW OF IT.

UNLESS IT IS SEEN, NO ONE CAN COMPREHEND THE HORROR. IT IS SURREAL... EVEN TO THOSE WHO LIVE THROUGH IT.

DISRUPTION OF ELECTRICITY CAUSES SPORADIC RADIO AND T.V. TRANSMISSION. BUT... THEY GO ON.

WHAT USED TO BE A GREAT NEWSPAPER NOW CONSISTS OF ONLY A FEW PAGES. DESPITE A LACK OF WATER... POWER... MATERIAL... THEY GO ON.
OSLOBOĐENJE
7

DEATH AND DESTRUCTION ARE PERVASIVE... AND IRONY PLAYS COUNTER-POINT TO THE MORBIDITY OF A GHASTLY WAR.
JUST MARRIED

TO MAINTAIN SANITY, ACTS OF SEEMING INSANITY OCCUR. SHREIKING SHELLS ARE INTERTWINED WITH MUSIC FROM STREET MUSICIANS.

AND IN THE APARTMENT THAT HOUSES ERVIN AND HIS FAMILY...
I MUST GET THIS FAX OUT TO MY FRIENDS ...BEFORE THE ELECTRICITY GOES OFF AGAIN.

I-I DON'T KNOW FOR SURE IF THEY WILL RECEIVE IT. OR... IF THEY CAN HELP.
BUT I MUST KEEP BUSY. KEEP MOVING.

WITHOUT HOPE-- THERE WOULD BE NOTHING!

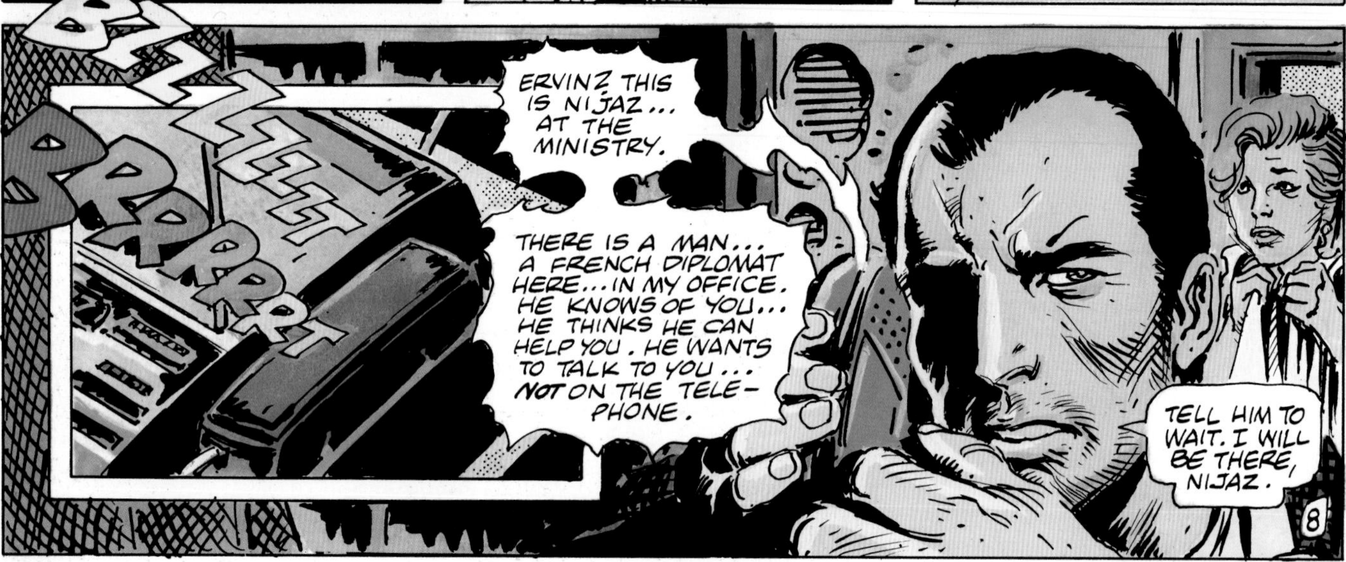
BZZZZTTT
BRRRRRT
ERVIN? THIS IS NIJAZ... AT THE MINISTRY.
THERE IS A MAN... A FRENCH DIPLOMAT HERE... IN MY OFFICE. HE KNOWS OF YOU... HE THINKS HE CAN HELP YOU. HE WANTS TO TALK TO YOU... NOT ON THE TELE-PHONE.
TELL HIM TO WAIT. I WILL BE THERE, NIJAZ.
8

I HAVE TO GO INTO THE CITY, EDINA. THIS MAY BE OUR CHANCE–
I KNOW. P-PLEASE BE CAREFUL, ERVIN.
EARLY DAWN... AGAIN ERVIN RUNS THE GAUNTLET...
BWEEEEEEOW
ZING
BEEEEOW
ZIP
ZING
ZIP
KCHUNG

TEN MINUTES LATER, THE BATTERED OPEL SPEEDS PAST THE HOLIDAY INN HOTEL TOWARDS THE MINISTRY IN SARAJEVO...

EVERY MINUTE WE REMAIN, EDINA AND THE KIDS ARE IN DANGER... FOR THEIR LIVES. I MUST GET THEM OUT...
75

ERVIN...THIS IS M'SIEUR LANGER...
WE HAVE HEARD A GREAT DEAL ABOUT YOU, MR. RUSTEMAGIC.
YOU HAVE MANY FRIENDS... GOOD FRIENDS.
9

M'SIEUR LANGER... I KNOW HOW DIFFICULT IT IS FOR ANYONE TO LEAVE SARAJEVO. ONLY THE CRITICALLY WOUNDED MAY BE FLOWN OUT.
THAT IS TRUE... AND YET... IT IS IMPORTANT THAT BOSNIA SHOULD SURVIVE.
NOT ALL CAN GET OUT... NOT ALL WANT TO GET OUT. BUT SOME OF YOU MUST GET OUT. TO HELP THE OTHERS.

I WAS BORN IN SARAJEVO. MY FAMILY... MY CHILDREN. I HAVE LOST MY HOME... MY BUSINESS. ALL GONE.
BUT... THERE ARE MANY OTHERS FAR WORSE OFF–

ERVIN... ESCAPE FROM SARAJEVO HELPS FOIL THE SERB PLANS FOR ETHNIC CLEANSING.
ETHNIC CL–? I NEVER EVEN KNEW IF I WAS A MUSLIM ...OR A CATHOLIC... OR WHAT.

THE PEOPLE I KNOW ALL MY LIFE... THAT I GREW UP WITH.. CROATS, SERBS, MUSLIMS, JEWS, CATHOLICS...
...I NEVER ASKED THEIR ETHNICITY. NOR DID THEY ASK IT OF ME! I - I DON'T UNDERSTAND.
ALL THAT YOU MUST UNDERSTAND IS THAT YOU MUST SURVIVE.

AM I INTERRUPTING? AH... THIS MUST BE ERVIN RUSTEMAGIC.
COME IN, JELENA.. COME IN.
10

JELENA IS ASSISTANT IN THE OFFICE OF IMMIGRATION.
DO YOU KNOW, MR. RUSTEMAGIC, THAT IN ORDER TO LEAVE SARAJEVO, CERTAIN FORMS MUST BE FILLED, FILED, AND APPROVED?
AND THAT OFFICIAL PERMITS CANNOT BE ISSUED BY ANYONE IN THIS ROOM.
GOOD-BYE.
DON'T BE DEPRESSED, ERVIN. JELENA IS A GOOD PERSON. SHE IS UNDER TERRIBLE PRESSURE... FROM THE SERBS... THE BOSNIAN PEOPLE... THE U.N....

GO BACK TO DOBRINJA, ERVIN. WE WILL CONTACT YOU AS SOON AS WE LEARN ANYTHING OF A DEFINITE NATURE.
THANK YOU, NIJAZ.. M'SIEUR LANGER. GOOD-BYE.

WHAT SHALL I DO? SARAJEVO IS MY HOME. YET... MY HOME DOESN'T EXIST ANYMORE.
EVERYTHING I'VE WORKED FOR ALL MY LIFE IS GONE!

EDINA IS CRYING ALL THE TIME... AND WHY SHOULDN'T SHE? SHE IS WORRIED ABOUT THE CHILDREN ...ABOUT ME...

...AND IF WE TRY TO GET OUT... WHO KNOWS IF WE CAN? MORE AND MORE PEOPLE DIE EVERY DAY.
11

CARLSEN

TELEFAX MESSAGE TO
Ervin Rustemagic
FROM
Andreas C. Knigge
DATE
23.07.92
PAGES INCL. THIS
1

Dear Ervin,

Although we have been trying since some time to get a fax through to you without any success so far, I am writing to you with the hope that the lines may be better this evening. I write to you with tears in my eyes. I have never been to your offices, but I have seen pictures from it in some brochures. I thought so often during the past weeks how you would feel in case they would be stolen or destroyed. Now all this has happened.

Think how it will be when you will finally see all your friends again. It's true that nobody can help you in this very moment, but you are not alone.

Take care, Ervin!

SARAJEVO,
26/07/1992
TO:
ANDREAS
KNIGGE

Dear Andreas,

I received well your July 23, fax yesterday and was very pleased to read it. My wife Edina couldn't avoid to cry after your nice and encouraging words.

I absolutely agree with your view of the things. However, I know that, if it happens that we survive this dirty war and get away from this hell one day, I will very often think about many things that are gone forever.

But, believe me that I'll try to concentrate to the words in your letter and that I'll try to start thinking that way. That's the only reasonable way, because like Joe said: "I have no options and no other choices".

Hope to see you all in the near ~~fut~~ future!

Dear Muriel and Joe,

Sarajevo, July 28, 1992

While I'm writing this, Edvin is watching Karate Kid Two on a neighbour's video. Edina and Maja are with him, laying on the floor, because shooting and shelling is not stopping since yesterday morning. Six people were killed and 21 wounded yesterday in our district of Dobrinja only. A friend just told me on the phone that they can't move inside a nearby building, because a sniperist shoots on everything that moves. That sniperist wounded a nurse in their building, while she was helping a wounded man.

Yesterday was 114th day of this siege of Sarajevo, and a friend here said that: "One would get fed up if he was spending a 114-day holiday in Hawaii".

I'm worried about after-war period here. I'm afraid that there will be no normal life.

Lots of love

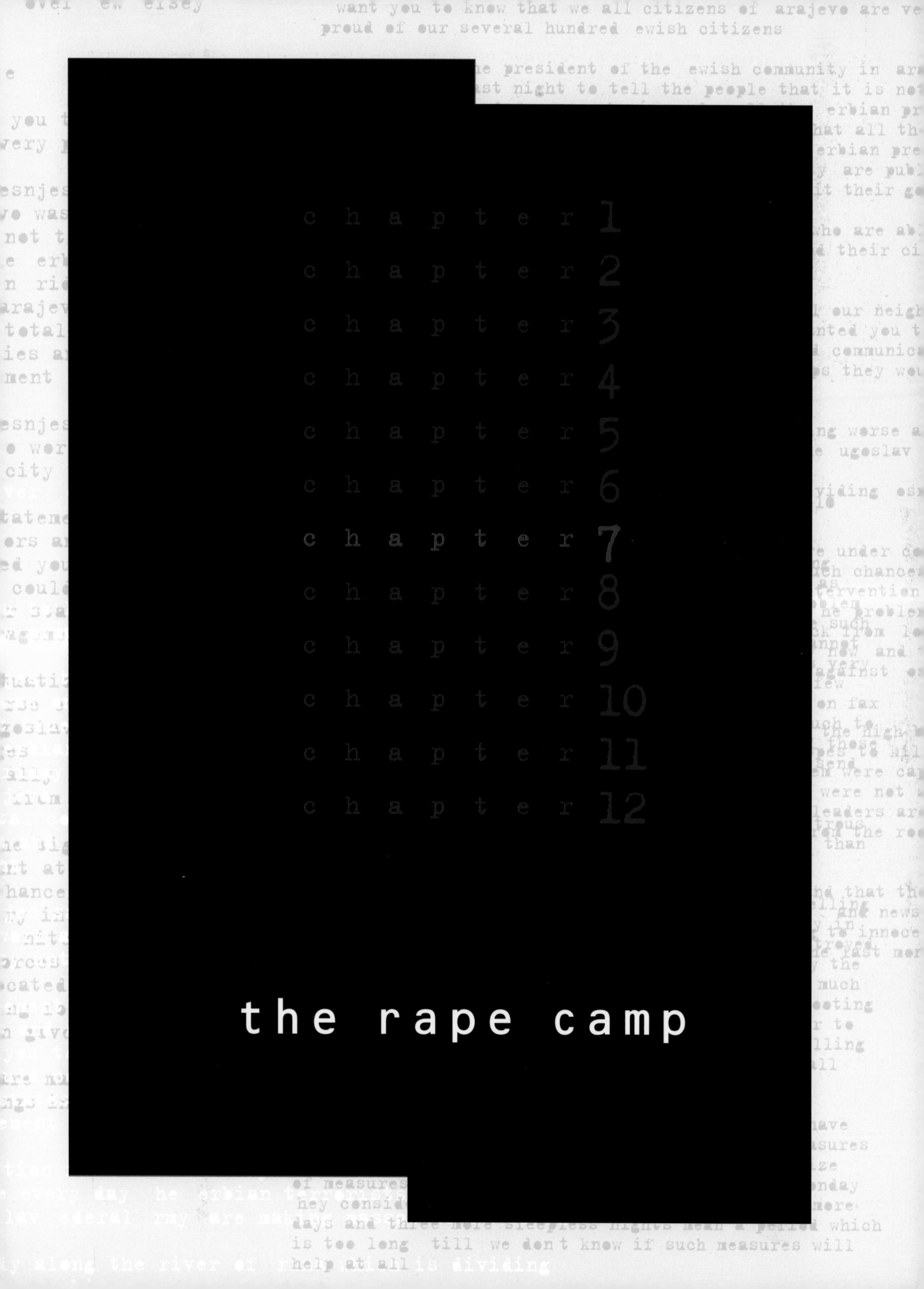
chapter 1
chapter 2
chapter 3
chapter 4
chapter 5
chapter 6
chapter 7
chapter 8
chapter 9
chapter 10
chapter 11
chapter 12
the rape camp

Sarajevo, October 31, 1992
(Saturday morning)

Dear Hermann,

Yesterday morning, I sent a fax to the U.N. French colonel Francois and also talked to captain Lemont, asking them to check if these two people are in Sarajevo as you told me. And if they are, I wrote to the French U.N. colonel to examine the possibility to transport us from Dobrinja to "Holiday Inn" hotel today. Hotel is not far from the Presidency and we could overnight there, to make sure to be in the Presidency on Sunday morning. Captain promised to call me back in the afternoon for sure, but he hasn't done it yet, and I didn't receive any reaction to my fax from the colonel Francois either.

If I don't hear anything from anyone, I'll ask a friend to take us to the Holiday Inn hotel in his small car. It is a very risky way to go, but we will have to take that risk, because staying here is as risky as well (last night a grenade hit our building a few meters above our apartment).

Love,

Ervin

IT'S NEAR THE END OF OCTOBER.. GETTING COLD. WINTER IS COMING. NO HEAT... WATER...

HOW MANY **MORE** TIMES MUST I MAKE THE RUN INTO THE CITY? WHAT WILL HAPPEN TO EDINA.. IF I AM HURT? AND THE CHILDREN? WHAT BECOMES OF THEM?

IT'S SO LATE... AND I AM SO TIRED. MAYBE TOMORROW I—

EDINA. WHAT'S WRONG? WHO-
THANK GOD YOU'RE BACK SAFE, ERVIN.
YOU REMEMBER MY FRIEND, SAMIRA. SHE ARRIVED ONLY HOURS AGO...

I DID NOT KNOW WHERE TO TURN. YOUR FATHER TOLD ME WHERE YOU WERE, EDINA. HE SAID TO TELL YOU ... HE IS WELL.
I-I AM SO **ASHAMED**.
YOU AND I KNOW EACH OTHER ... SINCE WE WERE CHILDREN. YOU MUST TELL ERVIN WHAT HAPPENED, SAMIRA. **EVERYTHING**.
IT- IT WAS **HORRIBLE**, EDINA. WORSE THAN **DYING**.
2

THE SERB SOLDIERS CAME TO OUR FARM... ON THE OUTSKIRTS OF DOBRINJA.
OUR FAMILY HAS ALWAYS LIVED THERE. MY MOTHER ...FATHER. MY BROTHER. IN SPITE OF THE WAR, WE WOULD NOT LEAVE. IT IS OUR HOME.
THE CHETNIKS CAME. ANIMALS! DIRTY SWINE!
THIS IS YOUR SON? WHO ELSE IS IN THE HOUSE? YOU HAVE WOMEN?
ONLY MY WIFE AND DAUGHTER. BUT... WHY-?
WE HAVE A NEED FOR THEM. THEY WILL COME WITH US.
WH-WHAT NEED? WHERE-?
KLICKT
NO CONCERN OF YOURS. WE HAVE NO NEED OF YOU!

3

UNHH... PAPA..

H-HE... IS BLEEDING. HELP HIM.. PLEASE...
HE.. IS DYING.

NO. HE IS **DEAD.**
DRAGAN. **DO IT..** WITH YOUR KNIFE.

URGHH.

YOU TWO ARE MOST **FORTUNATE.** YOU WILL BE PERMITTED TO **LIVE...**

... AND YOU WILL HAVE THE HONOR OF BEARING **SERB CHILDREN.**

THE FATHERS OF YOUR CHILDREN STAND BEFORE YOU... **NOW.**
4

MURDERERS! H-HAVEN'T YOU... DONE ENOUGH?
LEAVE MY DAUGHTER ALONE-
SILENCE! YOUR DAUGHTER WILL EXPERIENCE A MAN. A SERB OFFICER.
COME, GIRL.

I WILL TAKE THE GIRL INTO THE OTHER ROOM. AFTERWARD, WE DELIVER THEM TO THE CAMP... FOR THE PLEASURE OF OTHERS.

DO WITH THE MOTHER AS YOU WILL... BUT GAG HER. I WANT NO DISTRACTIONS.

"I COULD HEAR MY MOTHER'S MOANS. I FELT NOTHING. I COULD ONLY SMELL THE STINK OF THE MAN ON TOP OF ME."

WE WERE FINALLY TAKEN OUT... PAST THE BODIES OF MY FATHER... MY BROTHER.
INTO THE TRUCK WITH OTHER WOMEN. GIRLS. CHILDREN. ALL WITH BLANK, STARING EYES.
5

THEY TOOK US SOMEPLACE... TO A CAMP... ALL WOMEN.
TO MAKE US PREGNANT WITH SERB CHILDREN.
HOW... DID YOU ESCAPE, SAMIRA?
WITH GOD'S HELP ...AND A GOLD RING. A GIFT.. FROM MY FATHER.
A YOUNG SERB SOLDIER. ONLY A BOY.
M-MY MOTHER.. IS DEAD. MY FATHER... MY BROTHER...
I HEARD YOU WERE HERE.
STAY WITH US, SAMIRA.
N-NO. I HAVE FAMILY. I CAME ONLY TO WARN YOU. B-BE CAREFUL... FOR YOURSELF. AND MAJA.

SOME FOOD, SAMIRA? WATER..?
NO, EDINA.. I MUST GO.
TAKE CARE OF YOUR FAMILY, ERVIN... THE WORLD IS INSANE.
I MUST GET MY FAMILY OUT OF SARAJEVO.
6

Sarajevo, November 1, 1992

Dear Hermann,

Sarajevo was under constant fire and shelling the whole day yesterday (14 people killed, 109 injured). Therefore we didn't go to the Holiday Inn hotel. At 9 P.M. yesterday the French colonel telephoned, refering to my fax. He told me that we're doing it the wrong way and that French Government is taking wrong steps in our evacuation. The first step should be to contact UHNCR (U.N. High Commitee for Refugees). I told him: "If French Government doesn't know, how could I know?". They promised that they will do their best but there can be problems because it is being done the wrong way. So, we will have to stay here today and wait for phone calls and infos.

At 2 o'clock this morning Edina got up. She didn't feel well and asked me for some water. I gave her a glass of water, and while I was trying to light up a candle, she went to the bathroom. The same second I heard a strong and painful scream and then she fell down on the floor. I tried to lift her, but there was no sign of life in her body anymore. Her eyes were blank and she had a frightening grimace in her face. While I was washing her face, Maja went to the neighbour's door and was knocking heavily to wake them up. Neighbours came in one minute and took care of Edina. My friends doctors were here in five minutes and gave Edina some cocktails of injections. She came back to the consciousness, but her blood pressure was very low (90/70).

It is 210 days today since this war started, and we spent them in the real center of hell, Edina lost 20 kg in these seven months, and did not go outside at all. We were eating mostly rice and bread. And the last two months were full of tension, because we were waiting to be evacuated. However, the last week was extremely tensive. First we got the news about Dr. Dubin and started to pack up, but he didn't show up. Then Serbs attacked Jajce and masssacred women and children who were on the run. United Nations sent their 2856th warning to Serbia . . . Then you informed about Dr. Charpy and Dr. Vernant and we got excited again . . . And yesterday Serbs started a full scale artillery attack on Sarajevo. Edina was smoking too many cigarettes yesterday and almost didn't eat anything at all. So, her collapse was a result of all that together. It was too much for a human being! She is a little better this morning. Still, doctors said that she can go on the trip.

EDINA... YOU **MUST** REST.
I'M... ALL RIGHT. THE CHILDREN NEED ME. **YOU** NEED ME...

THERE WILL BE **PLENTY** OF TIME TO REST, ERVIN. AFTER WE -
PRRRTT
PRRRTTTT

HELLO. WHO-?
ERVIN? IT'S ME. NIJAZ. AT THE MINISTRY.
I HAVE SOME NEWS... FROM MARTIN ...IN HOLLAND.
YES, YES... I'M LISTENING.
I TRIED TO FAX HIS MESSAGE TO YOU...BUT...YOUR MACHINE DID NOT ACCEPT IT.
THE ELECTRICITY WAS DOWN. READ IT TO ME, NIJAZ.
MARTIN SAYS THERE IS A FRENCH OFFICIAL WHO MAY BE ABLE TO HELP YOU.
THE FRENCHMAN WILL BE HERE-- IN SARAJEVO-- WITHIN THE NEXT FEW DAYS...TO GET YOU OUT.
YES, YES. WHAT DOES MARTIN WANT ME TO DO?
YOU **MUST** BE IN THE CITY... WITH YOUR FAMILY...READY TO **LEAVE...** WHEN HE GETS HERE.
8

WHAT IS IT, ERVIN?
WE HAVE A CHANCE TO LEAVE ...BUT...

..IT HAS TO BE FROM SARAJEVO. WE MUST GET INTO THE CITY.

IT-IT IS DANGEROUS TO GET THERE. THE CHILDREN-

MAYBE IF YOU ASKED ONE OF YOUR COMIC-BOOK SUPER-HEROES, HE COULD FLY YOU INTO SARAJEVO.

GRANDPA! LOOK, MAMA. IT'S GRAND-PA!

PAPA! WHAT ARE YOU DOING HERE? HOW-?
I WALKED. NEIGHBORS TOLD ME WHERE YOU WERE STAYING.
9

EDINA... I HEARD YOU WERE GOING TO LEAVE... EVACUATE.
I WANTED TO SEE YOU...THE CHILDREN. BEFORE-
COME WITH US, PAPA.
NO, EDINA. I AM AN OLD MAN... I WILL **NEVER** LEAVE SARAJEVO... NO MATTER WHAT. IT IS MY **HOME**.

I JUST WANTED TO SEE YOU... TO SAY GOOD-BYE.
TO YOU. TO ERVIN. TO THE CHILDREN.
THIS HAS BECOME A WORLD OF **POLITICAL HYPOCRITES**.
THEY SAID THE HOLOCAUST SHOULD NEVER HAPPEN AGAIN. AND, YET... THEY **PERMIT** THIS KILLING TO GO ON. THEY TALK... AND SAY NOTHING. DO NOTHING.
NO ONE WILL HELP, PAPA. WE CAN DEPEND ONLY ON **OUR-SELVES**.
I **WILL** GET EDINA AND THE CHILDREN OUT... I PROMISE.
GOOD. NOW... I MUST GO.
LISTEN TO YOUR MOTHER AND FATHER, CHILDREN. AND STAY WELL.

WHREEEEEEEEEEEE
KRUMPF

P-PAPA...?

11

FROM '01 10/11 11:30 P.02

Sarajevo, Nov. 21, 1992

Dear Martin,

My friend Nijaz called me yesterday morning and said: "I've got a nicely typed fax from Martin for you". However, due to some problems with the electric aggregate in the Dobrinja Hospital, he couldn't fax it to me here before late in the afternoon, which is the reason why I'm writing to you only this (Saturday) morning.

Everything sounds great, but, like you said, we must not get excited too much about it. Just everything went wrong so far, and we had too many stresses on with everything else. We can't afford more stresses!

Exiting Dobrinja by car is still a very risky venture. Between 2 and 4 people get killed and about a dozen are wounded every week on the "barricade of death", which represents a column of trucks lined up along a part of the road which is under a constant fire of Cetniks. However, that's the only way one has to take when he drives to the city.

So, the best place for us to meet Mr. Kouchner would be, of course, the Dobrinja Hospital. The building in which we're staying is only 50 meters far from the hospital. I could bring our luggage to the hospital in the morning of Friday the 27th, and we could watch the hospital through the window of the apartment. When we see the U.N. vehicles approaching the hospital, we will run downstairs and will be there in only one minute. We could also stay and wait inside the hospital, but it is absolutely the same thing.

I'll try to get a letter from the B-H Government written in English. As soon as the letter is ready, we will fax it to you, so that you can forward it to the French government officials. Let's hope they make it in Sarajevo next week, after three months and a half, and after so many cancellations of his visits which were announced in the meantime.

Love,

Ervin

12

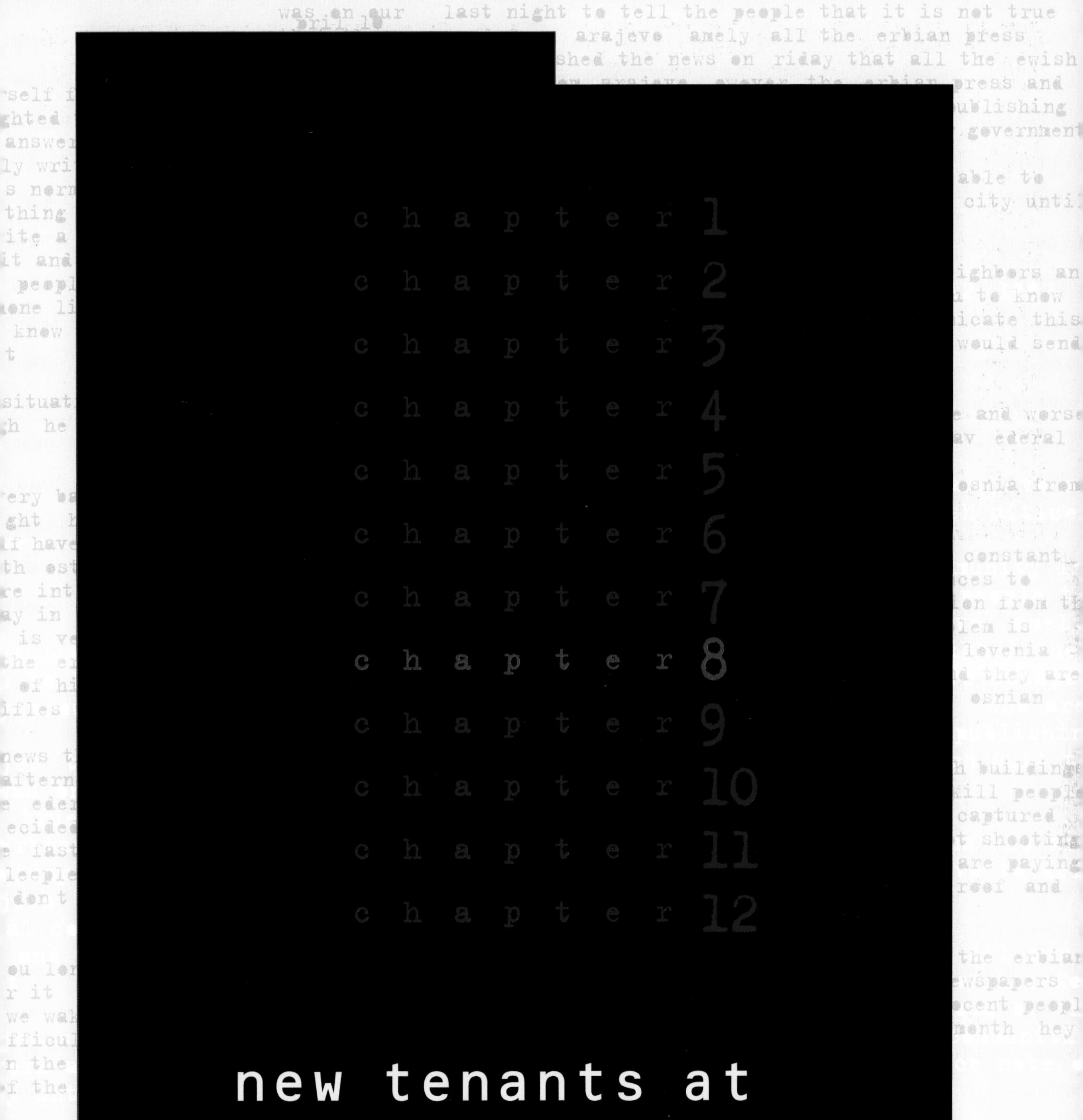

new tenants at the holiday inn

NIGHT... IN THE BATHROOM OF A SHELL-TORN BUILDING IN DOBRINJA...
BRRRRRT
BRRRRRRRT
A FAMILY SUCCUMBS TO SLEEP DESPITE THE DULL THRUM OF EXPLOSIONS THAT ERUPT WITH METRONOMIC CADENCE.

WHO? NIJAZ. IT'S THE MIDDLE OF THE NIGHT. WHAT-?

WHO WAS THAT, ERVIN?
NIJAZ. AT THE MINISTRY. WE MUST GET TO THE CITY IMMEDIATELY.
A FRENCH MINISTER IS EXPECTED ...WE ARE TO BE EVACUATED.

DRESS THE CHILDREN WARMLY, EDINA.
TAKE ONLY WHAT YOU CAN CARRY.
WE MUST RUN TO THE HOSPITAL.
MINUTES LATER...
...SOMEONE TO DRIVE US INTO THE CITY, DOCTOR. CAN YOU HELP US?
OF COURSE, ERVIN.
1

THEY'RE TAKING US OUT OF SARAJEVO, DOCTOR. WE GAVE OVER OUR APARTMENT TO ANOTHER REFUGEE FAMILY.
MIRZA WILL DRIVE YOU AND RETURN WITH THE CAR. GOOD LUCK TO YOU, ERVIN... STAY WELL.
W-WILL WE ALL BE ABLE TO GET IN? THE CAR IS SO SMALL-
NO MATTER. IT'S A SHORT RIDE.

THE COMIC BOOKS ARE NOT FOR READING, EDVIN. PUT THEM IN YOUR SHIRT... OVER YOUR HEAD. YOU, TOO, MAJA...
WHY, PAPA?

JUST DO AS I SAY, EDVIN. GOOD, MAJA.
GET THE CHILDREN DOWN LOW, EDINA.
WE'RE READY, MIRZA.
GET SET, ERVIN. HERE.. WE.. GO!

AGAIN, THE BATTERED OPEL KADET ROARS DOWN THE GAUNTLET OF BLISTERED TRUCKS... AMIDST THE STACCATO OF AUTOMATIC GUNFIRE...
SPLUNNK
BRWEEEEEEEE
SPLANG
SA★244-196
BWEEEEEEEEEE
VREEEEEEE

AS EVENING SETTLES OVER THE BESIEGED CITY OF SARAJEVO...
WE MADE IT, MIRZA... THE MINISTRY IS JUST AHEAD.
YES, ERVIN. YOU'RE ON YOUR WAY.
SOON, YOU WILL FORGET THIS TRAGEDY. LIVE A NORMAL –
FORGET? YOU JOKE, MIRZA. I COULD SOONER FORGET TO BREATHE.
GOOD-BYE, MIRZA. TAKE CARE.
YOU, TOO, ERVIN.
'BYE
WE ARE HERE TO SEE THE FRENCH DEPUTY.
HE IS NOT HERE. WE DO NOT EXPECT HIM.

HE... MAY HAVE BEEN DETAINED.
IS IT ALL RIGHT IF WE WAIT... HERE... IN THE LOBBY?
OF COURSE. THERE... ON THAT BENCH.
OH, ERVIN.. I AM AFRAID–
DON'T WORRY, EDINA. WE WILL... WAIT.
3

ANYTHING COULD HAVE HELD HIM UP. THE SERBS KEEP BOMBING THE AIRPORT...

...MAKING IT IMPOSSIBLE TO LAND. HE'LL COME...
...BUT... I WON'T LET MYSELF BECOME TOO OPTIMISTIC...

..THE DIS-APPOINTMENT, THEREFORE, WOULD BE LESS.
I MUST NOT BE TOO NEGATIVE, EITHER. FOR EDINA'S SAKE. FOR THE CHILDREN.

BUT... WHAT IF HE DOESN'T COME? WHAT DO WE DO?
W-WE CANNOT GO BACK TO DOBRINJA. AND EVEN IF WE COULD... THERE IS NO PLACE FOR US.

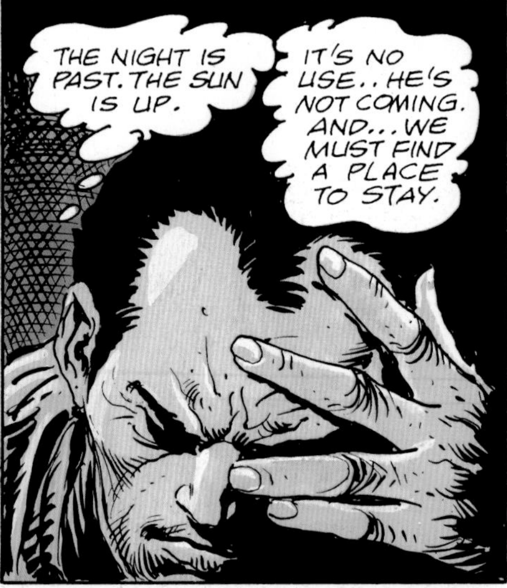
THE NIGHT IS PAST. THE SUN IS UP.
IT'S NO USE.. HE'S NOT COMING. AND... WE MUST FIND A PLACE TO STAY.

COME, EDINA... WAKE THE CHILDREN. WE... MUST LEAVE... THE MINISTRY.
H-HE DIDN'T COME, ERVIN?

YOU'RE WALKING TOO... FAST... PAPA.
I'M SORRY, MAJA.
DO YOU WANT ME TO CARRY YOU, EDVIN?
I'M... FINE, PAPA...
4

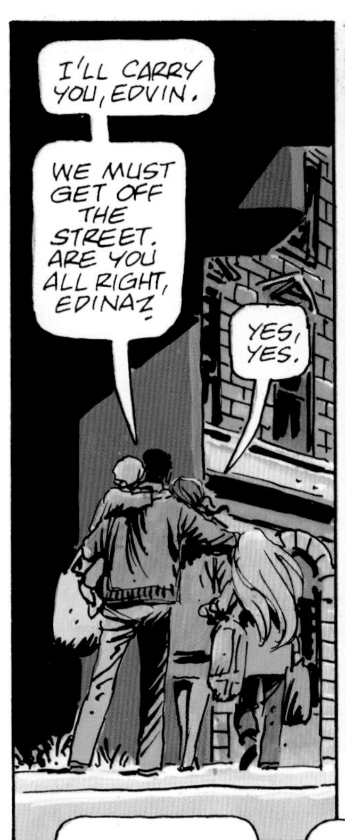
I'LL CARRY YOU, EDVIN.
WE MUST GET OFF THE STREET. ARE YOU ALL RIGHT, EDINA?
YES, YES.

THE HOLIDAY INN HOTEL IS JUST A FEW BLOCKS AWAY.
I KNOW THE MANAGER OF THE HOTEL. IF WE CAN GET A ROOM..

...EVEN FOR A DAY OR TWO... UNTIL THE FRENCH DEPUTY ARRIVES.

ARE WE GOING TO STAY AT THE HOTEL, PAPA?
I HOPE SO, MAJA... I DO HOPE SO.

THIS IS THE PLACE WHERE THE NEWS MEDIA STAY TO REPORT ON THE WAR.
IT WILL NOT BE EASY TO GET A ROOM.

IS IVANKA TRIVIC HERE? I HAVE TO SPEAK TO HER -
I'M SORRY. SHE WAS WOUNDED BY FLYING GLASS. SHE IS IN THE HOSPITAL...

I NEED TO HAVE A ROOM... FOR MY FAMILY.

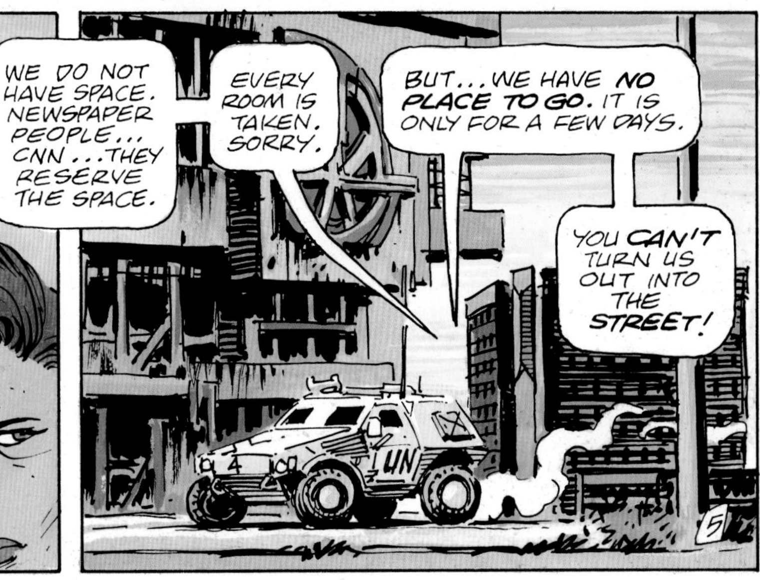
WE DO NOT HAVE SPACE. NEWSPAPER PEOPLE... CNN... THEY RESERVE THE SPACE.
EVERY ROOM IS TAKEN. SORRY.
BUT... WE HAVE NO PLACE TO GO. IT IS ONLY FOR A FEW DAYS.
YOU CAN'T TURN US OUT INTO THE STREET!
UN

FAX: 31-10-473 8586

SARAJEVO, 28.11.1992
AFTERNOON, 4 P.M.

DEAR MARTIN,

IT IS EXACTLY 24 HOURS AS WE'RE WAITING IN THE PRESIDENCY AND THERE'S NO SIGN OF THE FRENCH DEPUTY YET. THE AIRPORT IS CLOSED AFTER 4.30 P.M. I'M WORDLESS AND CAN'T WRITE MORE. I BOOKED A ROOM IN THE „HOLIDAY INN" HOTEL, ROOM NO. 420. WE WILL HAVE TO STAY THERE TONIGHT, BECAUSE THERE'S NO WAY TO GET BACK TO DOBRINJA TODAY.

LOVE,
Ervin

6

Sarajevo, November 29, 1992
Sunday, 29. 11. at 11.40 A.M.

Dear Martin,

At 11.00 A.M. I received your fax of yesterday evening, from which I understood that you didn't receive my two faxes. One was sent on Friday evening (in that one I confirmed that we arrived to the Presidency building at 4 P.M.). In my fax of yesterday afternoon I wrote to you that, after spending 24 hours in the Presidency, we're going to the HOLIDAY INN hotel. This second fax was sent to you around 5 P.M.

This is what has happened: On Thursday evening telephones became dead in Sarajevo and didn't work the whole day. On Friday morning I was waiting till 3.00 P.M. for a message. We left to go to the Presidency. We kissed everybody for "good bye" and left Dobrinja at 3.30 P.M. We arrived to the Presidency at 4.00 P.M. They allowed us to wait there the whole night, in the lobby. So we did the next day until 4.00 P.M., when we decided to book a room in HOLIDAY INN hotel, because we didn't feel well (especially Edina and Maja . . . Children suffered the most and were very hungry. . . I was in the Presidency again this morning at 9 o'clock. At 11 A.M. I received your fax of yesterday.

To tell and to explain to you how I feel, is useless now. However, what worries me now the most is how to tell this to Edina. I will probably leave it until I return to the hotel.

Your sentence "if you could only get to Split" sounds ridiculous (sorry) at this end! If we could only get to Kiseljak, a place which is 20 km far from here, we could reach New York or Tokyo from there easily (if we only had the permission to enter Croatia, of course!).

All we need is the permission from UNHCR in Geneva. Everybody is telling me that they just can't understand why we were dirrected to B. Ghali in New York. The persons who decide on who can and who cannot leave Sarajevo by plane are: Mrs. Sadako Ogata, Mr. Cyrus Vance and Lord Owen and they all are in Geneva!!!

Still, I don't know what to say. In spite of everything, I think that the French government still didn't send an official request to UNHCR in Geneva. We can be faxing each other for ages, or as long as we're still alive here, but if the most important thing is not done, everything seems to be useless. If we get that permission from UNHCR in Geneva, we can go by one of their planes the next day. There is no need to wait for someone to come and takes us with him.

Now we have another problem: when we left Dobrinja, we had to sign that we were leaving the apartment which we were using as refugees for good (that is the procedure). Now we don't know if we can go back there. It could very well be that a new family of refugees moved in there already.

I'll try to phone after this fax,
but I can talk only 2 minutes

Love,

Ervin

"IT NEVER CEASES TO AMAZE ME... HOW PEOPLE CAN ADAPT TO ALMOST ANYTHING... NO MATTER HOW FATE TWISTS OR TURNS."
"A YEAR AGO, I WOULD HAVE THOUGHT IT IMPOSSIBLE TO LIVE THIS WAY. IN CONSTANT FEAR OF BEING CAUGHT IN THE SIGHT OF AN UNSEEN MARKSMAN ...OR... THE VICTIM OF AN UNDISCRIMINATING GRENADE."
NOW.. IT'S JUST A PART OF NORMAL LIFE.

"UP MARSHALL TITO STREET... PAST THE CENTRAL BANK BUILDING ...INTO THE MINISTRY."
I AM ERVIN RUSTEMAGIC.
THEY'RE EXPECTING YOU. GO RIGHT IN.
THANK YOU.

COME IN... AH, MR. RUSTEMAGIC. I'M GLAD YOU'RE HERE. NIJAZ HAS TOLD ME MUCH ABOUT YOU.

YOU AND YOUR FAMILY WILL ACCOMPANY ME ...TOMORROW... WHEN I LEAVE SARAJEVO.

FOR NOW, GO BACK TO YOUR HOTEL. I WILL CONTACT YOU... BEFORE I LEAVE.
NOW... I MUST ATTEND ANOTHER MEETING.

WHAT DO YOU THINK, NIJAZ?
GO BACK TO YOUR HOTEL... AND WAIT. HE WILL CONTACT YOU. I BELIEVE HIM.
8

IF OUR LUCK HOLDS... MAYBE—
MR. RUSTE-MAGIC. A MOMENT.
YOU REMEMBER ME? JELENA. WE MET IN NIJAZ'S OFFICE... A FEW DAYS AGO.
AS I TOLD YOU AT THAT TIME... PERMISSION TO LEAVE SARAJEVO MAY BE OBTAINED ONLY FROM UNHCR* IN GENEVA.
NO MATTER WHO SAYS DIFFERENTLY, THAT IS THE WAY IT IS DONE. IT IS A MISTAKE FOR YOU TO RAISE FALSE HOPES. GOOD-BYE.
*UNITED NATIONS HIGH COMMITTEE FOR REFUGEES

I-I'VE GOT TO GET BACK TO THE HOLIDAY INN.
HOW AM I GOING TO EXPLAIN THIS TO EDINA?

ARE YOU ALL RIGHT, ERVIN? YOU LOOK TIRED. WHAT.. DID THEY SAY...?
THERE IS A CHANCE, EDINA.
HOW ARE THE CHILDREN?
THEY'RE ASLEEP.
WHAT'S THAT EDVIN HAS IN HIS BED?
A PUPPY. POOR THING. HE FOUND IT IN THE HALL-WAY. I DON'T KNOW HOW WE'LL FEED IT—
IT'S ALL RIGHT. EDVIN NEEDS IT... WE'LL WORK IT OUT.
9

COME TO BED, ERVIN.
SOON, EDINA. FIRST, I WANT TO WRITE SOME FAXES.

NIJAZ SAID HE WOULD SEND FOR ME.
I'VE GOT TO LET MARTIN AND THE REST KNOW WHAT'S GOING ON.

THEY'RE ALL TRYING TO HELP US. CONTACTING GOVERNMENT OFFICIALS... CONSULATES... THE U.N.

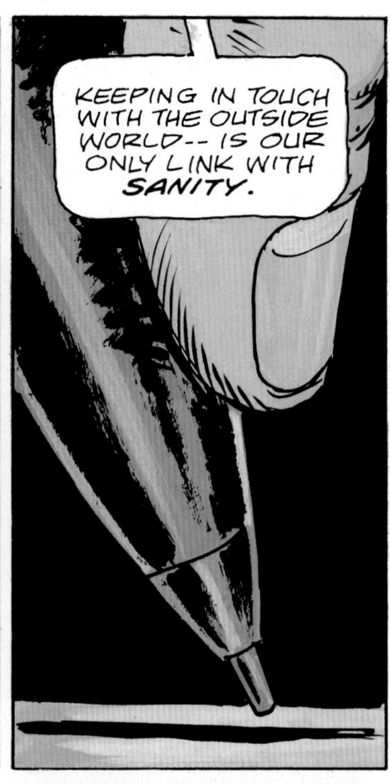
KEEPING IN TOUCH WITH THE OUTSIDE WORLD-- IS OUR ONLY LINK WITH SANITY.

NEXT MORNING..
GOOD MORNING, ERVIN. I GOT FOOD FROM THE HOTEL KITCHEN. SOME BREAK-FAST...?

LOOK AT ALL THE PEOPLE RUNNING TO THE HOTEL, EDINA. I WONDER-

THE HOTEL MANAGER SAID THAT THEY RECEIVED A SHIP-MENT OF CIGAR-ETTES TODAY.

FOR THE NEWS-PEOPLE, MAINLY, AND TO SELL SOME TO THE "CIVILIANS."
10

SNIPER FIRE! SOMEONE'S BEEN SHOT!

H-HIS HEAD. THE BLOOD-
GET HIM OFF THE STREET!
INTO THE HOTEL. HURRY.

TH-THAT MAN WAS KILLED... ONLY... BECAUSE HE WANTED A CIGARETTE.

11

Sunday, 28. 11. 92 at 4:00 P.M.

Dear Martin,

The French Minister of the Humanities arrived to the Presidency at 2.30 P.M. Thanking to Nijaz who came there, too, I was allowed to be presented in the meeting room.

He smiled, made his arms wide open and brought me close to him for a very strong hug, like if we knew each other for ten years:

"Finally! I'm so happy to see you! People were calling me about you every two days in the last six months. I'm glad that I can take you with me now!".

After that he went to another room, for another meeting. Dr. Vernant left the crowd, took me to a corner and said:

- You can't go just like that! You need a permission from UNHCR in Geneva

- But you heard what the Minister just said?!?

- Yes, but he doesn't know it. He doesn't have the power to take you without the permission from Geneva!

That woman is a real beast, worse than any kind of snake. She talked to me in such an unpleasant and such an enemy way that I never experienced it before in my life.

When the Minister finished his second meeting, I came to him again. I told him that I am becoming to be worried because his collaborators are telling me that they have to get a permission from Geneva. The Minister asked them: WHY ?!?

They made hell of an effort to explain that he is a French minister and that he can't break the U.N. rules just like that . . .

The Minister said - If they say NO, I'll talk to them personally - I got a feeling that he was saying this only because I was present. I don't believe that he will do it and I don't think that we will go with them tomorrow.

Anyway, they asked me to stay in the Holiday Inn hotel with my family and to wait there. If they get the Geneva approval, they'll contact me.

They're leaving tomorrow. We will wait here, but I'm sure we're not going.

Love,
Ervin

P.S. The Minister left Sarajevo withouth us.

12

c h a p t e r 1

c h a p t e r 2

c h a p t e r 3

c h a p t e r 4

c h a p t e r 5

c h a p t e r 6

c h a p t e r 7

c h a p t e r 8

c h a p t e r 9

c h a p t e r 10

c h a p t e r 11

c h a p t e r 12

attempt to cross the airport

DECEMBER 5, 1992

DEAR MARTIN,

I spoke to a French colonel this morning by phone. He will not help, because they could lose their credibility of "neutrality". At the end of our conversation he told me:

- I wish you and your family all the luck in your running across the airport's run-a-way. And if you make it alive to Paris, you will have a lot of questions to ask your minister-friends!

- What do you mean by that? - I asked.

- Well, I was there when the Minister told you that he's taking you with him and then he didn't do it.

He added that before the Frenchman left Sarajevo he was asked by one of his assistants: "Shall I send a car to pick up Mr. Rustemagic and his family in Holiday Inn?" . . . The answer was "No!".

So, the minister who embraced me didn't forget about me. He just didn't want to take us with him. Their explanation about their need "to contact Geneva" was only an excuse. If they really intended to take us with them and if they needed to contact Geneva, they could have done it before coming to Sarajevo and not when they were about to leave Sarajevo. And that embrace was only a part of a show . . . Nothing else but a circus show! Anyway, I find it useless and ridiculous now wasting time and satellite faxes in discussing it over and over.

Love,

Ervin

IN DORDRECHT, HOLLAND, THE CHUG-CHUG OF A STEAMER IS ACCOMPANIED BY THE CLATTER OF A FAX MACHINE...
IT'S FROM ERVIN. NOT GOOD.
...AT THE HOME OF WRITER MARTIN LODEWIJK.
I'LL TELEPHONE THE OTHERS. THEY MAY HAVE SOME IDEAS.
GOD--IT'S FRUSTRATING.

OUTSTANDING INTERNATIONAL CARTOONIST HERMANN...IN BRUSSELS...
YES, YES, MARTIN. WE MUST KEEP TRYING.

IN SWITZERLAND, AT THE HOME OF THE ARTIST, HUGO PRATT...
I WILL CALL THE MINISTER OF CULTURE IN PARIS...

IN DOETINCHEM, HOLLAND...
YES, MARTIN.. I HAVE USED EVERY PENNY IN ERVIN'S BUSINESS ACCOUNT HERE TO PAY FOR THEIR ROOM AT THE HOLIDAY INN..

SIX HOURS AWAY, IN DOVER, NEW JERSEY, U.S.A....
I'LL CALL A JEWISH ORGANIZATION I KNOW, HERMANN. THEY MAY HAVE CONTACTS IN SARAJEVO.

IN EAST FLATBUSH, BROOKLYN, U.S.A....
YES, JOE... I BELIEVE A GROUP IN LONDON IS HELPING EVACUATE JEWS.
I'LL TRY TO CONTACT THEM.
IN LONDON, ENGLAND.
YES, RABBI..WE ARE INVOLVED IN SARAJEVO. BUT, YOU SPEAK OF ONE FAMILY.
THOUSANDS ARE DYING... AND..THE WORLD DOES NOTHING.
2

JANUARY 24, 1993

DEAR MARTIN,

I appreciate all the efforts which Rabi Herschel Gluck is doing, but I just talked to the head of the Jewish organization in Sarajevo. He told me to forget about it, because they are not even thinking of organizing a new convoy before March! Still, I was advised not to go across the airport to Butmir, because he knows a number of people who tried it lately and just disappeared.

It is two months now as we're in Holiday Inn. We can stay few days more, but we can't keep paying bills the way we did it once. The hotel ask for cash only. It is so difficult explaining all these details this way !!!

Did you ask for a journalist's accreditation for myself? More than twenty people from Sarajevo got them from foreign newspapers and TV-stations (some work as translators for their journalists here) and they can fly in and out from Sarajevo regardless their nationality. The same goes for holders of foreign passports.

Love,

Ervin

(3)

DO YOU REALIZE WHAT YOU ARE SAYING, EDINA?
WE WOULD HAVE TO GO BACK TO DOBRINJA... PAST THE BARRICADE OF TRUCKS... THROUGH THE GAUNTLET OF SERB GUNFIRE.

THEN... THE AIRFIELD ITSELF. COVERED BY SERB CANNONS.. AND PATROLLED BY U.N. SOLDIERS. NEITHER WILL LET US PASS.

AND THE WEATHER GROWS COLDER. BELOW FREEZING AT NIGHT. THE CHILDREN DO NOT HAVE WARM CLOTHING, NOR DO WE. IT IS TEN MILES TO BUTMIR...
...IF WE GET ACROSS THE AIR-FIELD.

HOTEL
AT LEAST HERE... WE ARE REASON-ABLY SAFE, EDINA.
HMMPH. I CANNOT BELIEVE I SAID THAT.

ERVIN... WE HAVE NO CHOICE.
ALL RIGHT, EDINA. GET OUR PAPERS ...MONEY... ONLY WHAT WE CAN CARRY.
I WILL CALL THE HOSPITAL IN DOBRINJA.

AS THE SUN IN ITS DESCENT CASTS LONG SHADOWS ACROSS BOMB-SCARRED BUILDINGS...
THE CAR IS HERE, EDINA.
EDVIN... DID YOU GIVE THE PUPPY TO SOME-ONE?
YES, PAPA. TO MY FRIEND... ON THE NEXT FLOOR.
HELLO, UP THERE! ERVIN! IT'S ME... MIRZA. YOUR FAVORITE CHAUFFEUR.
HERE TO TAKE YOU BACK TO YOUR HAPPY HOME IN DOBRINJA.
4

I DIDN'T THINK I'D SEE YOU AND YOUR FAMILY AGAIN SO SOON, ERVIN.
WE MISSED YOUR PRETTY FACE, MIRZA.
CHUNGA CHUNG
CHAKACHAKA
TLING
VREEE
ZING
VIP ZIP
5A•244
PRETTY? YAH. SURE.
HOLD TIGHT, MY FRIENDS. STAY DOWN. WE'RE ALMOST THERE.

MID-FEBRUARY... THE RETURN TO DOBRINJA...
WE MADE IT. WHAT IS HOLDING THIS OPEL KADET TOGETHER, MIRZA?
SPIT, WIRE... AND A PRAYER, ERVIN.

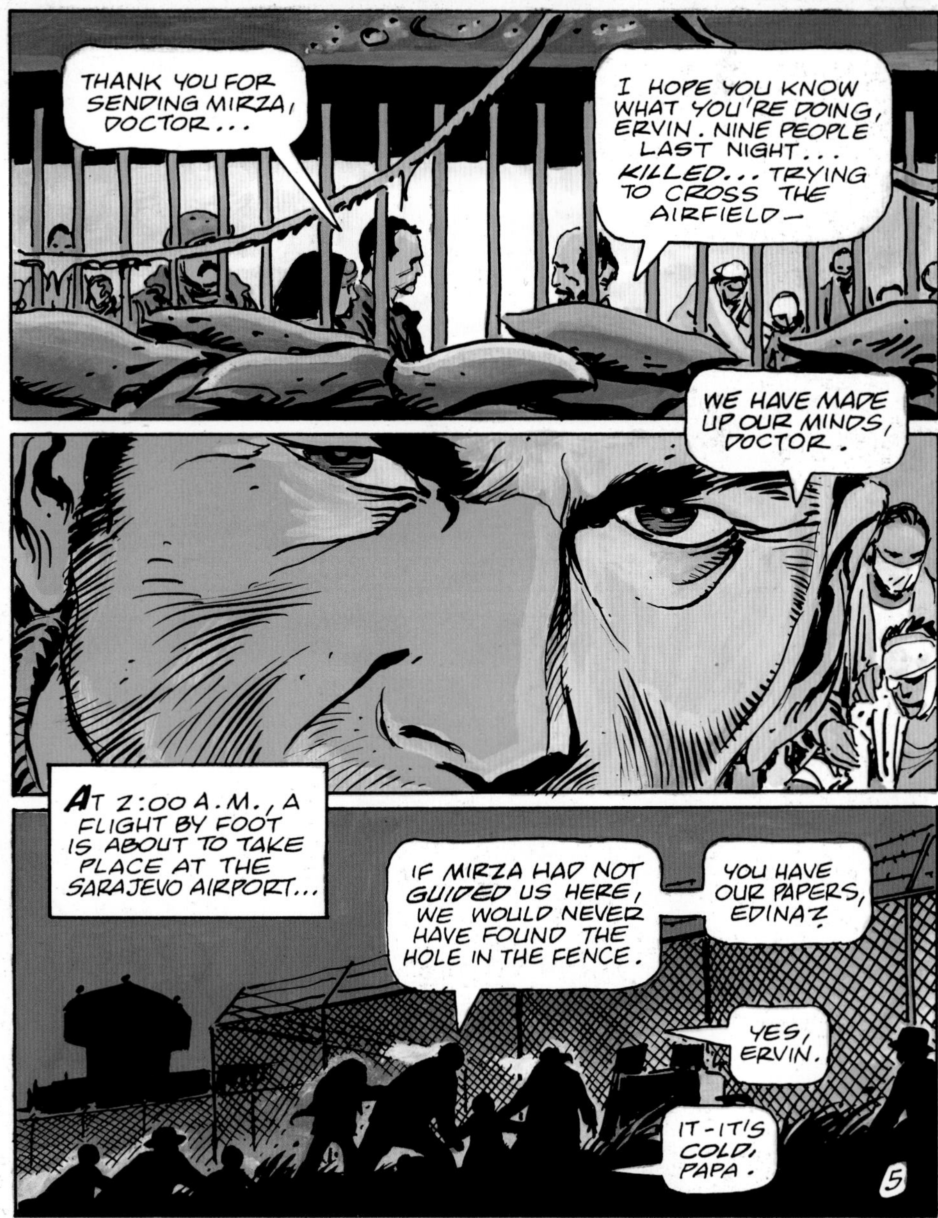
THANK YOU FOR SENDING MIRZA, DOCTOR...
I HOPE YOU KNOW WHAT YOU'RE DOING, ERVIN. NINE PEOPLE LAST NIGHT... KILLED... TRYING TO CROSS THE AIRFIELD—
WE HAVE MADE UP OUR MINDS, DOCTOR.
AT 2:00 A.M., A FLIGHT BY FOOT IS ABOUT TO TAKE PLACE AT THE SARAJEVO AIRPORT...
IF MIRZA HAD NOT GUIDED US HERE, WE WOULD NEVER HAVE FOUND THE HOLE IN THE FENCE.
YOU HAVE OUR PAPERS, EDINA?
YES, ERVIN.
IT-IT'S COLD, PAPA.
5

WE ARE NOT THE ONLY ONES HERE, EDINA... OTHERS ARE MAKING THE CROSSING...
MY HEART... IS BEATING... LIKE A DRUM. HARD TO BREATHE.
S-STAY CLOSE TO ME, MAJA.
HOLD MY HAND, PAPA.

WE MUST CROSS THE ROAD... GO THROUGH THE DITCH... THEN, UNDER THE FENCE.
RUN!

UNDER THE TORN WIRE, EDVIN... QUICKLY. STAY TOGETHER. HOLD MY ARM, MAJA.
ARE YOU ALL RIGHT, EDINA?
Y-YES :GASP:
IT'S STARTING TO SNOW, PAPA...
STAY CLOSE TO ME, EDVIN. THE U.N. SOLDIERS PATROL THE FIELD... AND THE SERB CANNONS SIGHT IN FROM THE HILLS. WE MUST RUN—
SPOTLIGHTS! DOWN ON THE GROUND --AND DON'T MOVE!
6

BWEEEEEEEE
TZINNG
KEEP YOUR HEADS DOWN!
PEOPLE RUNNING. BUT... THEY ARE GOING... THE WRONG WAY.
BEEEEEOW

I-I CAN'T BELIEVE IT. THEY ARE CARRYING BOXES... BAGS... COCA-COLA.
SOMEONE IS HIT.
THEY RISK THEIR LIVES ...TO BRING IN FOOD.
I'M COLD. MY TOES ...ARE F-FROZEN, PAPA.
HOLD ON, EDVIN... HOLD ON.

WE MUST STAY STILL. IF WE MOVE... THEY WILL SHOOT AT US.
HOLD ON.

AFTER WHAT SEEMS LIKE HOURS...
THEY'VE STOPPED FIRING. CRAWL FORWARD SLOWLY...

STAY CLOSE TO MAMA, MAJA. HOLD ON TO ME... AND RUN, EDVIN. WE ARE ALMOST ON THE OTHER-

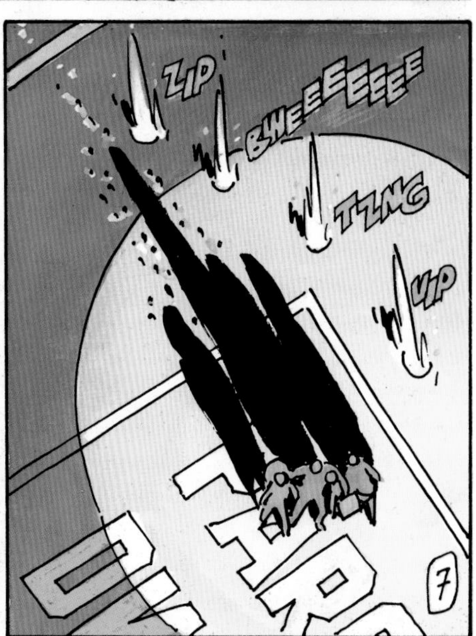
ZIP
BWEEEEEEEE
7

RATATAT TCHUNGA
BAM CRACK BLAM CHUNG
CEASE FIRE!
STAND UP!
P-PLEASE..LET US THROUGH. MY WIFE IS SICK... MY CHILDREN ARE FREEZING.
THE AIRPORT IS OFF-LIMITS. YOU ARE LUCKY YOU WERE NOT SHOT!
GO BACK NOW!
P-PAPA... MY FEET... ARE S-SO C-COLD.
MY TOES HURT..
ARE THEY... GOING TO KILL US, MAMA?
NO, MAJA.. BUT, WE MUST GO BACK.
WE MUST GET BACK TO THE HOSPITAL, EDINA.
YES, ERV-
OH, MY GOD! I- I DON'T HAVE IT!
8

WHAT IS IT? WHAT'S WRONG?
OH'GOD... I - I MUST ... HAVE DROPPED IT!

M-MY POCKET-BOOK... WITH OUR MONEY. PASSPORTS. I DROPPED IT... ON THE AIRFIELD.
STAY WITH THE CHILDREN, EDINA. I'LL GO BACK—
NO! IT'S TOO DARK... YOU'LL NEVER FIND IT. THE GUARDS WILL SHOOT—
D-DON'T GO, PAPA...

THAT WAS ALL THE MONEY WE HAVE. AND... WE NEED THOSE PAPERS FOR ANY CHANCE TO GET OUT.
STAY HERE, EDINA. WAIT FOR ME... HERE.

I... CAN'T SEE A THING. WAIT—
THE SPOT-LIGHT.

WH-WHAT'S THIS? I CAN'T BELIEVE IT.
EDINA'S WALLET!
9

PAPA... IT'S PAPA!
ERVIN! THANK GOD...
I FOUND IT, EDINA. I FOUND IT.

IT'S A SIGN, ERVIN. OUR LUCK... IS CHANGING.
ARE WE SAFE, PAPA?
M-MY FEET... ARE SO COLD...
WE WILL GO BACK TO THE HOSPITAL. STAY CLOSE TO THE BUILDINGS...
IT'S ALMOST DAWN. THE SNIPERS WILL BE AT WORK.
TELEFON
ERVIN... I THOUGHT YOU WOULD BE ALMOST IN BUTMIR BY NOW. WHAT HAPPENED?
WE ARE LIKE THE PROVERBIAL BAD KOPEK, DOCTOR. WE KEEP TURNING UP.
PLEASE, DOCTOR ...LOOK AT EDVIN'S FEET. IT MAY BE FROSTBITE...
10

EDVIN IS FORTUNATE. HIS TOES WILL BE OKAY. IT'S WINTER, YOU KNOW, ERVIN...
BOOTS WOULD BE WARMER THAN SNEAKERS.
IT TICKLES.

ARE THE SHOE STORES OPEN THIS LATE, DOCTOR? I'LL GO SHOPPING–
VERY FUNNY, ERVIN.
YOU AND YOUR FAMILY STAY HERE TONIGHT. YOU ALL NEED TO SLEEP. REST...

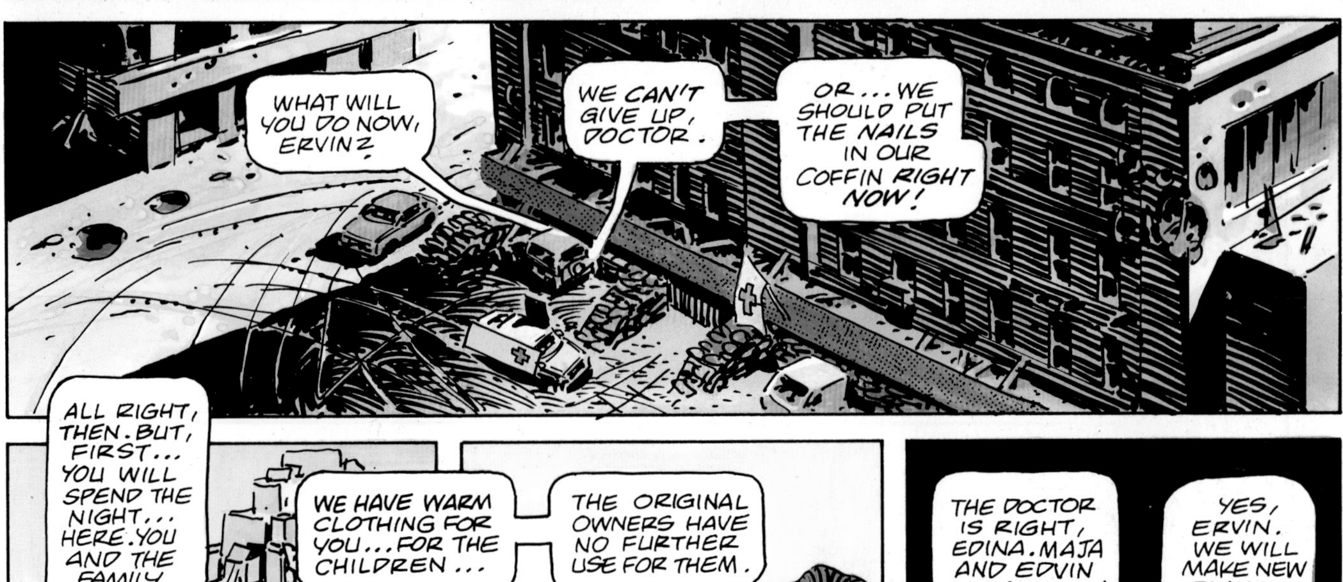
WHAT WILL YOU DO NOW, ERVIN?
WE CAN'T GIVE UP, DOCTOR.
OR... WE SHOULD PUT THE NAILS IN OUR COFFIN RIGHT NOW!

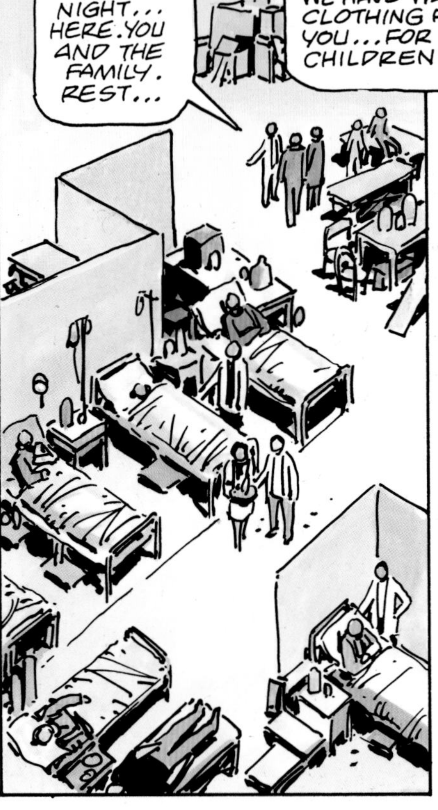
ALL RIGHT, THEN. BUT, FIRST... YOU WILL SPEND THE NIGHT... HERE. YOU AND THE FAMILY. REST...

WE HAVE WARM CLOTHING FOR YOU... FOR THE CHILDREN...
THE ORIGINAL OWNERS HAVE NO FURTHER USE FOR THEM.

THE DOCTOR IS RIGHT, EDINA. MAJA AND EDVIN ARE ALREADY ASLEEP...
YES, ERVIN. WE WILL MAKE NEW PLANS... TOMORROW.
11

January 29, 1993

Dear Muriel and Joe,

"Some people die too early, some die too late. It is still not usual in this world that some people die in the right moment ".

Well, tens of thousands of people who died in Bosnia in the last ten months died too early. A child died yesterday in the mother's stomach, killed by a grenade, twenty days before it was born.

I didn't experience any other war before this one, but I don't believe that there was a more cruel war in the world's history. One million five hundred thousand grenades exploded in the city of Sarajevo (three grenades per each citizen) so far and nobody will be able to count how many millions of bullets were shot. This is a barbaric siege of a city on the door step of 21st century.

You know I never say "thank you" to friends. But this only time I want to make an exception and to thank you for all nice moments we had from you in the most difficult period of our lives. And whatever happens to us, we want you to know that we will love you very much forever.

DADO MAJA Aina ERVIN

January 29, 1993

Dear Hermann,

Some people say that every war has its good sides. So far the only good side of this war was that we learned how to make a candle from the kitchen oil, how to listen to the radio-transistor if there is no electric power or batteries and how to wash in one litter of water . . .

When I think of it sometimes . . . We had everything we needed. A nice house and nice offices. And when I remember how I was doing it with much love and with much care, wanting to have a nice place to live and a nice and comfortable place to work. But now, everything is gone, and I'll have to start all over again, if we survive this war. However, we're still alive and should count ourselves lucky so far.

Still, you can't escape from thinking: "If I did this, if I did that . . ." If we knew that this was going to happen we could have sold our house, my office, my mother's house, and moved anywhere in Europe. However, I try not to think about all that. I have to concentrate only on how to get out from this hell.

But, shall we ever be able to tell you how much we love you? Although you are physically far away, you were closer to us than you will be ever able to imagine . . . I will describe to you how much it means to us. I'll try . . . if I only make it to Brussels ever again . . .

Love,

DADO MAJA Aina ERVIN

Sarajevo, January 29, 1993

Dear Martin,
I could write a book about this war, but I'm not going to. There are too many aspects of it, and it would be hell of a work.

One of the aspects of this war is that you don't really live your life, although you're getting older faster. We have a total blockade here and we don't even know which are new books, new movies, new songs or new car types. Also, you forget to behave as a normal human being. We don't use the door bell anymore, because we have electricity so seldom. Knocking is the only way before entering a house. My god, how much one can regress being absent from the civilized world for one year only?!?

For ourselves this war is nothing else but a struggle for survival. I tried to read, but after reading a chapter, listening to the sound of bullets and grenades, you realize that you don't remember what you read.

How much it means to us keeping in touch with you all the time and receiving your satellite faxes. Whatever I say, it will not be strong enough to express all our feelings . . . So, how about this: "I wish the same barbaric war to take place in Holland and that you spend ten months in the siege of Rotterdam, so that I can do for you the same you do for us!" ?!?

Love to all of you,

MAJA Aina ERVIN DADO

WE MADE IT, ERVIN... BACK INTO THE CITY.
YES, MIRZA. AND... IN SPITE OF EVERYTHING...
...SARAJEVO LOOKS BEAUTIFUL IN THE SNOW.
DO YOU REMEMBER ...JUST A FEW YEARS AGO... WHEN THE WORLD OLYMPICS WERE HELD HERE?
PEOPLE CAME FROM ALL OVER THE WORLD TO SARAJEVO.
IT WAS LIKE A WONDERLAND.
SNOW-SKI CONDITIONS WERE MAGNIFICENT.
78
JOE KUBERT
ONE SUMMER BEFORE THE WAR, OUR FRIENDS FROM AMERICA-- JOE AND MURIEL-- VISITED US HERE.
THEY DRANK PURE WATER FROM THE SOURCE OF THE BOSNIA RIVER. OR WAS IT A DREAM?
2

WELL... THE HOLIDAY INN STILL STANDS ...AT LEAST.
THANK YOU, MIRZA, FOR-
JUST THANK GOD YOUR LITTLE TRIP ACROSS THE AIRPORT DID NOT END WITH WORSE RESULTS, ERVIN.

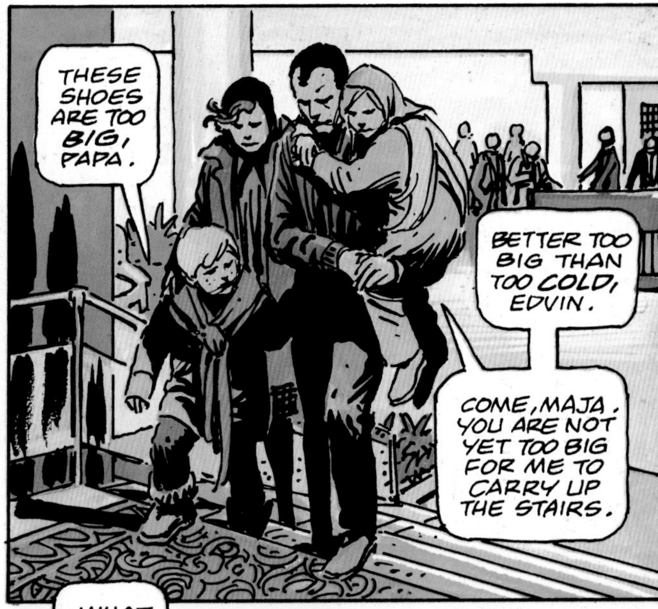

THESE SHOES ARE TOO BIG, PAPA.
BETTER TOO BIG THAN TOO COLD, EDVIN.
COME, MAJA. YOU ARE NOT YET TOO BIG FOR ME TO CARRY UP THE STAIRS.

IT'S A GOOD THING I DIDN'T CANCEL OUR ROOM, EDINA.
I HOPED WE WOULD NOT BE BACK... BUT... I DON'T WANT TO GO THROUGH THAT AIRFIELD EXPERIENCE AGAIN, ERVIN.
I WONDER IF I CAN GET MY PUPPY BACK?

WHAT DO WE DO NOW?
I-I DON'T KNOW. BUT.. WE HAVE MANY FRIENDS WHO ARE TRYING TO HELP US GET OUT.
MAYBE WITH A LITTLE LUCK, WE-

WHREEEEEEEEEEEEEEEEE
HOTEL
3

THAT SHELL HIT UP-STAIRS... IN THE OVERHEAD APARTMENT.
MAYBE SOMEONE IS HURT-

STAY HERE WITH THE CHILDREN, EDINA. I'LL GO SEE...

THEY'RE ALL... DEAD...
IT... COULD HAVE BEEN EDINA.
OR... THE CHILD-REN.
4

Sarajevo, February 17, 1993
Wednesday, 16.00 h

Dear Martin, Hermann, Joe,

We failed with our airport-Butmir trip, but are still alive. We arrived to the Dobrinja hospital yesterday. My friends Dr. Hajir and Dr. Fauzy were very reluctant about our attempt, because 8 people got killed and 13 wounded in such an attempt the night before. Still, we were determined to go . . . . with an experienced guide. The night was colder than previous ones, but we had hoped for the best . . . . walking across the main road and a piece of land, we entered the airport zone in about one hour. There we had to hide, lay on ground and crawl meter by meter, because French troops were circling around the runway in a dozen of armoured vehicles. Only in one place we had to lay on the frozen ground for some two hours until a nearby vehicle moved away. Edina and children were shivering. Our son's feet were frozen and he couldn't move. I had to carry him from then on. At 1 A.M we were near the Butmir's side of the airport's runway area (about 90% of the trip made) when French soldiers discovered us . . .

Our return from that point to Dobrinja was the most difficult part of that 7-hour agony. When we were running from there to the main road, Serbs noticed us and opened the fire from their Kula post. We jumped on the ground while anti-aircraft bullets were trilling above us. Twenty minutes later Edina realized that she lost her purse. She was pleading me to forget about it, but I crawled back and succeeded in finding passports, and some documents spread on the ground in the dark.

Edina and Maja were in total shock, but we managed to bring them back to the hospital around 2 o'clock. Doctors and nurses made them feel better after one hour. Maja felt very ill while Edina was only shivering. Edvin slept well. Nobody cares about bleeding knees or arms and legs which still ache very much.

Today at noon we returned to Holiday Inn. We missed a grenade for only 10 seconds. Edina and children are scared to death and they wouldn't try that airport-Butmir trip again for one million years. We find ourselves practically in no way out.

Obviously, our fate is to stay and die in Sarajevo with full support from the French ministers and officers.

Love,

Ervin

DORDRECHT...
HE WANTS MONEY, HERMANN. LOTS OF IT. WHAT SHALL WE DO?

BELGIUM...
DO, MARTIN? WE WILL GET THE MONEY... SOMEHOW. CALL HUGO AND JOE. SEE WHAT THEY CAN DO...

SWITZERLAND...
OF COURSE, MARTIN... I WILL HELP.

UNITED STATES...
YES, MARTIN... WE HAVE TO TRUST YOUR CONTACT. GO AHEAD WITH THE DEAL.

OKAY. YOU HAVE THE MONEY. ARE YOU SURE YOU CAN DO IT? LIVES DEPEND ON YOU–
DON'T WORRY, MY FRIEND... THEY ARE AS GOOD AS OUT.
I'LL LET YOU KNOW WHEN THEY ARE SAFE.
AND... DON'T CALL ME. I'LL CALL YOU.
WEEKS LATER, IN SARAJEVO...
IT'S A FAX FROM MARTIN, EDINA. THE MAN WHO WAS TO HELP US... HAS DISAPPEARED...
...WITH THE MONEY.
THAT DOES NOT LEAVE US WITH MANY OPTIONS... DOES IT, ERVIN?
NO, EDINA. AND WE DON'T WANT TO TRY CROSSING THE AIRFIELD AGAIN.
6

OUR FRIENDS ARE TRYING IN EVERY WAY TO HELP US... BUT... IT IS NOT WORKING.
WE CANNOT LOSE HEART. WE MUST NOT GIVE UP.

YES. FOR TWO VERY IMPORTANT REASONS.

AT THAT MOMENT... ON THE OUTSKIRTS OF AN OUTLYING VILLAGE NORTH OF SARAJEVO...
...DEFENSELESS, MALE CIVILIANS, YOUNG AND OLD... ARE LED INTO THE WOODS...

...AND SLAUGHTERED.

THE DEAD ARE COVERED...
...AS IF TO HIDE THE COLD HORROR FROM HEAVEN'S EYE...
...WHILE THOSE IMPRISONED ARE FATED TO DIE A SLOWER DEATH.

CHANGES IN CITY PLANNING TAKE PLACE IN SARAJEVO: SMALL PARKS BECOME NEW CEMETERIES. PLAYGROUNDS AND SOCCER FIELDS ARE EERILY ALTERED.

IT IS ONLY A MATTER OF TIME, EDINA ...BEFORE ONE OF US-
NO, ERVIN... YOU MUST NOT THINK OF IT.

THERE MAY BE A CHANCE... IF...

...IF I CAN GET OFFICIAL ACCREDITATION AS A NEWS CORRESPONDENT. NEWSPEOPLE MAY CROSS BORDERS... FREELY.
I MUST SEND A FAX... FROM THE MINISTRY.
8

I MUST SPEAK TO NIJAZ...AT THE MINISTRY.
THE STREETS ARE QUIET... FOR THE MOMENT.

I WOULD LIKE TO SEE NIJAZ.
SORRY.
NIJAZ LEFT SARAJEVO. YESTERDAY MORNING. WITH SIX COLLEAGUES. TO BUTMIR.

IS-IS HE COMING BACK?
NO. BUT, HIS ASSISTANT, NEDZAD, IS STILL HERE.

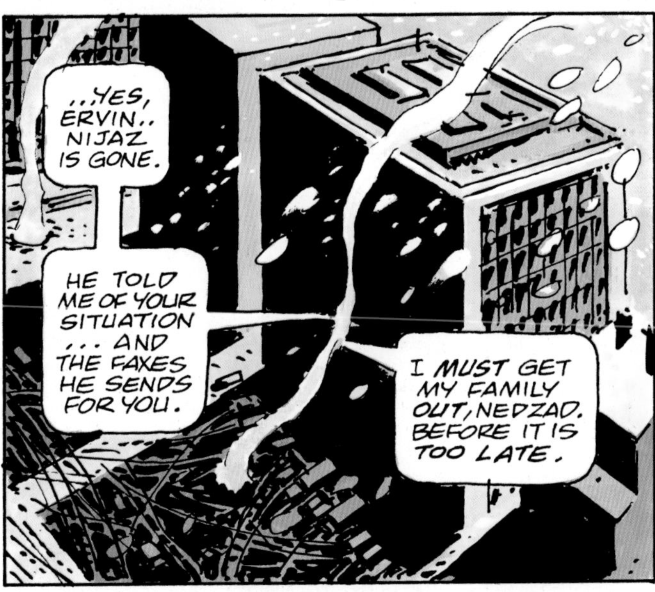
...YES, ERVIN.. NIJAZ IS GONE.
HE TOLD ME OF YOUR SITUATION ... AND THE FAXES HE SENDS FOR YOU.
I MUST GET MY FAMILY OUT, NEDZAD. BEFORE IT IS TOO LATE.

IT MAY ALREADY BE TOO LATE. FOR ALL OF US. SIX MONTHS AGO, NO ONE WAS THINKING OF LEAVING. BUT...

...THE U.N. CONTINUES TO DO NOTHING. LESS THAN NOTHING. AND THAT ENCOURAGES THE MURDERERS.
WHAT CHANCE DO I HAVE TO GAIN EXIT...AS A CORRESPONDENT?

IF I KNEW THE ANSWER TO THAT, I WOULD BE ON MY WAY OUT. THE RULES CHANGE BY THE DAY. BY THE HOUR!
IF AN UNPROFOR* OFFICIAL WILL GIVE APPROVAL ...OR... IF A COUNTRY ALLOWS YOU ENTRY...OR ...IF YOU ARE AN ACCREDITED CORRESPONDENT ...WHO KNOWS?
*UNITED NATIONS PROTECTIVE FORCE
9

OUR BOSNIAN PASSPORTS ARE OF LITTLE VALUE...
EVEN APPROVAL FROM UNHCR IS OF DOUBTFUL HELP.

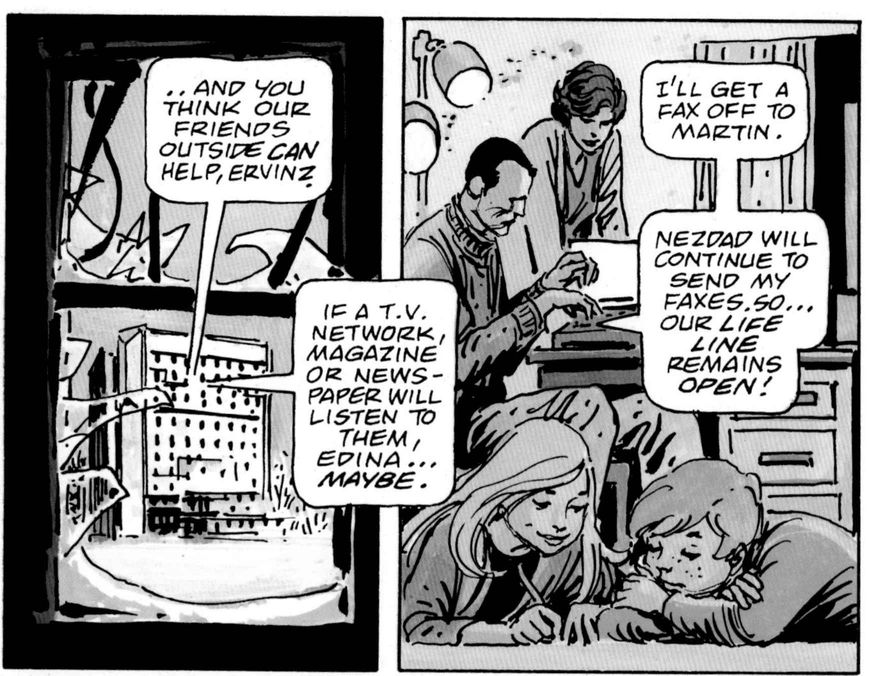
..AND YOU THINK OUR FRIENDS OUTSIDE CAN HELP, ERVIN?
IF A T.V. NETWORK, MAGAZINE OR NEWS-PAPER WILL LISTEN TO THEM, EDINA... MAYBE.
I'LL GET A FAX OFF TO MARTIN.
NEZDAD WILL CONTINUE TO SEND MY FAXES.SO... OUR LIFE LINE REMAINS OPEN!

DAYS CRAWL INTO WEEKS...
ERVIN? I HAVE A FAX FROM DORDRECHT. FROM MARTIN. I WILL READ IT TO YOU...

IT WAS FROM MARTIN. I HAVE NEWSMAN ACCREDITATION ...BUT...IT ALLOWS FOR ONLY ONE –
THEN AT LEAST ONE OF US WILL BE OUT-SIDE.
EVEN IF THEY DO LET ME OUT... HOW COULD I GO? HOW COULD I LEAVE YOU AND THE CHILDREN?
WHO BETTER THAN YOU TO GET US OUT?
ALL RIGHT, EDINA. IF I GET OUT... AND CANNOT GET YOU OUT WITHIN ONE WEEK... I WILL RETURN TO SARAJEVO.

IF YOU DO NOT GET US OUT WITHIN ONE WEEK... I WILL COME OUT AND PINCH YOU.
10

SATURDAY MORNING, APRIL 10, 1993...
...A U.N. ARMORED CAR APPROACHES THE HEAVILY GUARDED AIRPORT IN SARAJEVO.
UN
UN
MAKE SURE YOU ALL HAVE YOUR PRESS CREDENTIALS.
'TWILL BE JOLLY NICE TO GET BACK HOME.
PRESS
BE READY TO HAVE YOUR BAGS INSPECTED...
...INSIDE THE TERMINAL.

IS THIS ALL YOUR LUGGAGE, MR. RUSTEMAGIC? NOTHING MORE?
I HAVE LEFT EVERYTHING OF VALUE IN SARAJEVO.
YOU WILL ALL WAIT HERE, PLEASE. I WILL CALL YOU WHEN THE FLIGHT IS READY.
IN ABOUT FORTY MINUTES.

I DO HOPE THERE ARE NO MISTAKES. THAT BANGLADESHI SOLDIER COULD HARDLY READ.

MY WORD. THIS IS A BOARDING PASS. A PIECE OF NOTE PAPER WITH A NUMBER WRITTEN ON IT. TSK, TSK.

I HAVE NUMBER SEVEN...BUT...THERE ARE ONLY THREE OF US BOARDING. HOW-?

YOUR ATTENTION, PLEASE.
11

Sarajevo, March 5, 1993
Friday, 15.00 h

Dear Martin,

Nijaz left Sarajevo yesterday morning. UNPROFOR transported him and six more colleagues in an armoured vehicle to Butmir. He won't be back for a long time, but we can continue using the same satellite number. His secretary will be taking care of our faxes.

Most of our friends who weren't even thinking of leaving Sarajevo in October and November, when we were ready to leave, are gone now. Early in January Milan Trivic was making jokes about our evacuation and he told me: "Once, when you finally get out of here, please be so kind and organize my evacuation through your foreign connections". Well, he left Sarajevo one month ago, using UNPROFOR's press accreditation.

In some of my faxes I mentioned young artist Senad, who used to work in my office. In the past weeks he was drawing portraits of UNPROFOR's and UNHCR's officials. They were paying him in cigarettes, coffee, drinks and chocolates which they were purchasing in their tax-free shop. One week ago he did a portrait of Harry Hossingworth, a top official in Sarajevo's UNHCR. When he finished that drawing, Harry asked him how to pay for it and Senad answered: "How about a flight ticket to Split?". Harry promised to see what he can do. Next day he improvised a press accreditation for Senad and told him that he can fly to Split on Friday although Senad didn't have any other papers and permissions.

However, last night Senad came to see me and said that UNHCR brought a new rule which doesn't allow accredited journalists, holders of B-H passports, to go on their flights any more. In spite of that, Harry told him to come there in the morning, but "to be quiet about it".

This (Friday) morning I went, together with Senad, to the UNPROFOR's HQ building (UNHCR is located there, too). His flight permission was ready and he left for the airport at 10.00 h. The Press Office issued my UNPROFOR's press accreditation no. 10048. There I heard that UNHCR decided not to let anyone with B-H passport aboard their aircraft any more.

It was a pleasant 70-minute walk to Holiday Inn. It was snowing a lot, but wasn't that much shelling and shooting. When I arrived to the hotel and told Edina about new rules, she said: "I told you not to ask for that accreditation, because when you do, they will change the rules." . . . And they really did.

Love,

Ervin

12

c h a p t e r 1
c h a p t e r 2
c h a p t e r 3
c h a p t e r 4
c h a p t e r 5
c h a p t e r 6
c h a p t e r 7
c h a p t e r 8
c h a p t e r 9
c h a p t e r 10
c h a p t e r 11
c h a p t e r 12

ervin gets out

HOLIDAY INN

7671264376

Fax: 32-2-375 00 55

Sarajevo, February, 1993

Dear Hermann and Martin,

I'm sending you a short diary, so that you can have a follow up of the situation after you heard from me last:

FRIDAY, February 5, 16.00 h: I had a phone call from UNHCR. A girl told me that they got an ORDER from their headquarters in Geneva to check if I am still in Sarajevo. That girl was just calling our old number in Dobrinja when someone who happened to know that we're in "Holiday Inn" entered her office . . .

Geneva wanted to know how many members of family I have with me and the girl from UNHCR promised me that she will fax them at once all our details (names, birth dates, etc . . .). Then I tried to get in touch with the person in charge, but he wasn't in the office. So, I sent him a fax with this information.

SATURDAY, February 6, 11.00 h: Nothing new yet. I tried to call again. I was told that they received my fax and are on "stand by". As soon as the clearance from Geneva arrives, they will get in touch with me. I tried to call UNHCR, too, but couldn't get through.

SUNDAY, February 7, 12.00 h: Nothing new yet. We're very puzzled and do not know what to do. It's so difficult to decide . . . More than hundred persons tried to cross the airport's run-a-way last night. Six were killed and seven wounded.

TUESDAY, February 9, 11.00 h: Nothing yet. The girl in UNHCR becomes suspicious about this and so do we.

Love -
Ervin

DIDN'T QUITE MAKE IT OUT, EH, CLYDE?
'FRAID NOT. MAYBE TOMORROW.
GIN AND TONIC, PLEASE ...WITH A TWIST.

402
TAP TAP
ERVIN? H-HOW-?
THE FLIGHT ...WAS CANCELLED, EDINA.
COME INSIDE.

THE OTHERS...THE REPORTERS...WILL LEAVE TOMORROW OR THE NEXT DAY. I DON'T KNOW WHEN I WILL BE-
SHH... AS LONG AS YOU ARE SAFE, MY DEAR...
...THAT'S ALL THAT MATTERS, ERVIN.
Holiday Inn HOTEL
THE CHILDREN ARE ASLEEP. THEY WILL BE SO HAPPY... THAT YOU DID NOT GO.
EDINA... MAYBE I WON'T GET PERMISSION TO-
COME TO BED. YOU LOOK EXHAUSTED.
I-I AM TIRED, EDINA.
AND I AM SELFISH. BUT... I AM GLAD YOU COULD NOT LEAVE.
DESPITE HIS WEARINESS, ERVIN CANNOT SLEEP...

...AS HORRIBLE IMAGES INVADE HIS MIND. IMAGES THAT IMPERIL HIS WIFE AND CHILDREN.
2

YES... THIS IS ERVIN RUSTEMAGIC.
A MESSAGE? FROM THE MINISTRY?

April 14, 1993...
Mr. Rustemagic? A message here... for you.
Thank you.

Moments later, in their room..
Edina, they have space for me. I-I can leave-
How? When?

I must be down-stairs... in one hour. They are going to pick me up.
It has been months since-
Now is the time, Ervin. You must pack.
Money... your papers...

Within the hour the family huddles in the lobby of the Holiday Inn Hotel...
...as a light spring rain reflects in tearful good-byes.
I have been instructed to take you to the airport.
I'm ready.
UN

THE FACES OF HIS FAMILY ARE INDELIBLY ETCHED ON HIS MIND AS ERVIN IS DRIVEN THROUGH DOBRINJA . . .
UN
THE LIGHT PITTER-PATTER OF FALLING RAIN DOES NOT DISTRACT HIM . . .
W-WILL I GET OUT?
WILL I BE ABLE TO GET THEM OUT?
THE RAIN IS STOPPING.
THERE'S THE AIR-PORT. A TRANS-PORT IS ON THE TARMAC.
PLEASE HAVE YOUR PAPERS READY. VISAS... I.D. . . .
ERVIN! MY GOD. I THOUGHT YOU WERE DEAD...
NIGEL! WHAT ARE YOU DOING HERE?
I'M A JOURNALIST, YOU KNOW... FOR A GERMAN NEWSPAPER.
I HAVEN'T SEEN YOU SINCE WE MET IN APRIL OF '92 . . .
PRESS
ANOTHER APRIL... ANOTHER MEETING. IT'S A STRANGE TIME, NIGEL.
PLEASE PROCEED TO BOARD THE AIR-CRAFT . . .
WELL... HERE WE GO, ERVIN.
I CAN'T BELIEVE I'VE GOTTEN THIS FAR... WITHOUT A HITCH, NIGEL.
SOON WE'LL BE OUT OF THIS CRAZINESS, ERVIN. WHERE IS EDINA... THE KIDS?
5

...SO, ERVIN... EDINA AND THE KIDS ARE STILL IN SARAJEVO. WHAT WILL YOU - ?
U.S. AIR FORCE
I DON'T KNOW, NIGEL.
I HAVE FRIENDS IN SPLIT... I'LL FIGURE SOMETHING TO GET THEM OUT.
I'LL BE IN SPLIT FOR A WHILE, ERVIN... THEN, I'M GOING BACK TO SARAJEVO. IF THERE IS ANYTHING I CAN DO -
CBS
CNN
THANK YOU. YES. I'LL STAY IN TOUCH..
NOT BAD ENOUGH THEY GIVE US BOXES TO SIT ON... LOOK AT THESE HOLES IN THE FUSELAGE, ERVIN...
DIDN'T YOU HEAR THE SHOTS AS WE TOOK OFF? THAT WAS A FOND FAREWELL FROM THE SERB SNIPERS.
TH-THAT WAS CLOSE, ERVIN.
CLOSE, NIGEL... BUT, NO CIGAR.
MY BEAUTIFUL SARAJEVO. TORN ... BLEEDING.
EDINA... THE CHILDREN. DOWN THERE. HELPLESS. WHEN WILL I WAKEN FROM THIS DREAM?
6

FROM THIS HEIGHT THE LAND LOOKS SO PEACEFUL. NO HINT OF THE DYING... THE SUFFERING...
...FROM HERE, NO HINT OF THE MURDERED INNOCENTS THAT LIE... IN UNMARKED GRAVES.
WOMEN... CHILDREN... SLAIN. WITHOUT PITY. GOD! WHAT OF EDINA... TH-THE CHILDREN...?
LIKE A DARK WAVE, SORROW ...FEAR... LONELINESS.. ENGULFS HIM.
PRESS

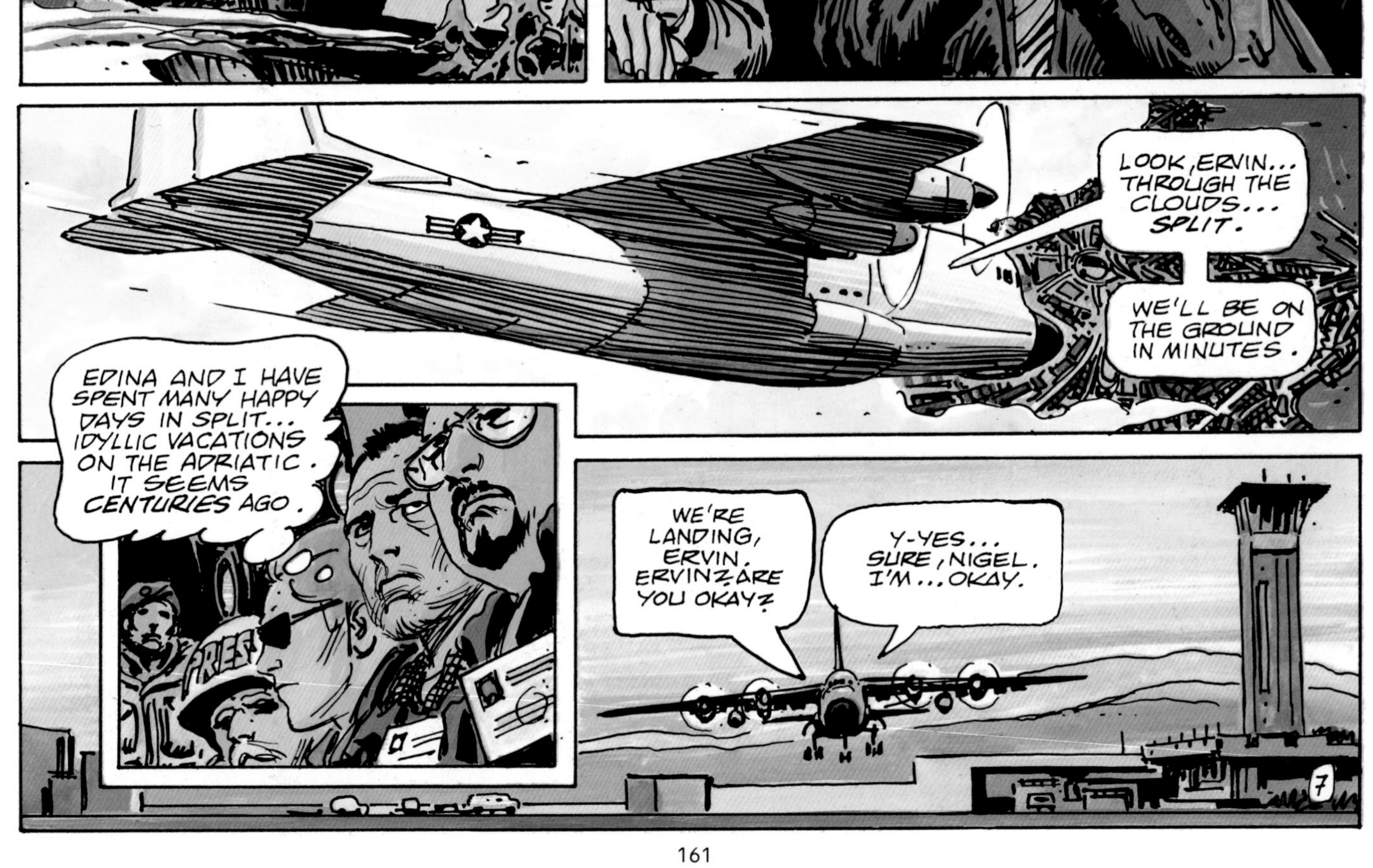
LOOK, ERVIN... THROUGH THE CLOUDS... SPLIT.
WE'LL BE ON THE GROUND IN MINUTES.
EDINA AND I HAVE SPENT MANY HAPPY DAYS IN SPLIT... IDYLLIC VACATIONS ON THE ADRIATIC. IT SEEMS CENTURIES AGO.
WE'RE LANDING, ERVIN. ERVIN?ARE YOU OKAY?
Y-YES... SURE, NIGEL. I'M... OKAY.
PRESS
7

I AM STAYING AT THE HOTEL MARJAN IF YOU NEED ME.
GOOD LUCK.
THANK YOU, NIGEL. GOOD-BYE.
THERE WAS AN ARTIST... TONY... WHO WORKED FOR ME IN SARAJEVO. HE HAD A HOME ...A WIFE... IN RIJEKA.
RIJEKA IS AN OVER-NIGHT FERRY RIDE FROM SPLIT.
NIGHT... ALONG THE ISTRIAN COAST OF THE ADRIATIC SEA...
WHAT WAS HER NAME? VERA. YES, THAT'S IT.
I ONCE VISITED THEM. THEY HAVE A HOUSE... CLOSE TO THE HARBOR IN RIJEKA.

DAWN... A LIGHT TAP ON THE DOOR OF A SMALL HOUSE IN RIJEKA...
HELLO, VERA... I -
ERVIN! WHAT ARE YOU DOING HERE? HOW DID YOU -

HOW STUPID OF ME! COME IN... I'M SO GLAD TO SEE YOU...

SIT, ERVIN... LET ME GET YOU SOME-THING TO EAT.
IS TONY HERE?
Y-YOU HAVE A CHILD. I DIDN'T KNOW...
YES... IVAN IS TWO YEARS OLD. B-BUT, TONY IS IN SARAJEVO.
HE WENT BACK TO HELP HIS MOTHER AND FATHER.
8

VERA...THINGS ARE NOT GOOD IN SARAJEVO. BUT, TONY CAN TAKE CARE OF HIMSELF.
AT LEAST HE KNOWS YOU ARE OUT OF HARM'S WAY.
WITH ME... IT'S THE OPPOSITE. I'M OKAY... BUT, EDINA AND THE KIDS ARE-
WHAT WILL YOU DO, ERVIN?
DO? ANYTHING! EVERYTHING! I-I WILL GO TO ZAGREB. I KNOW PEOPLE THERE...WHO MAY BE ABLE TO HELP ME.
IF I CAN GET TO ZAGREB.. OR ROME...
I PRAY TO WHATEVER GOD THERE IS THAT EDINA... IS STILL SAFE.
I HAVE NOT READ A NEWSPAPER IN MONTHS... ALTHOUGH OSLOBODJENJE IS STILL PUBLISHED AND PRINTED IN SARAJEVO.
ERVIN..I WISH I COULD-
WAIT. WHAT'S THIS?
AN AD. MY FRIEND, NEVEN IS IN POREČ ... NOT FAR FROM HERE.
A WARM BUT QUICK GOOD-BYE, AND THE ODYSSEY CONTINUES.
ZAGREB
NEVEN WAS A TRAVEL AGENT IN DUBROVNIK. NOW... HE IS IN BUSINESS IN POREČ.
HE WILL HELP ME... IF HE CAN.
SARAJEVO
RIJEKA
POREČ
SPLIT
DUBROVNIK
ADRIATIC SEA
9

Wednesday, April 14, 1993

Dear Muriel and Joe,

SURPRISE! I just put the phone down after talking to Ervin! He had just arrived in SPLIT!! Finally something went right! Incredible as it seems. The authorities have again changed the regulations for allowing accredited journalists to fly out of Sarajevo but Ervin slipped out between changes. Probably while they were phoning through the new orders. But he wasn't too excited about his "escape" as he is now very worried about Edina and the kids. He is much less optimistic about the possible convoy and very much expects that he will have to go back to Sarajevo to join his family again in a week or ten days time. So let us all pray for another miracle like this that brings out ALL the Rustemagics! He asked me to tell you, Hermann and Ali, but keep it to yourself. Just in case he DOES have to go back.

Maybe his luck has finally changed ?!

He could only be on the phone for a few moments but will try to call back this evening.
I'll keep you posted!

All the best,

MARTIN

edina and the kids get out

Zagreb (Croatia), May 20, 1993

Dear Martin,

I'm back to Zagreb again. On Saturday I will be in Split and there I'll decide if and when I'll go back to Sarajevo.

It is 36 days today since I left Sarajevo and arrived to Split. I couldn't do anything for Edina and children in that period of time and there are no chances that I can do something if I stay longer. I wish I never left Sarajevo, because it could have made the life easier for them and myself in the past month if I stayed there.

Serbs were shelling Sarajevo yesterday and three grenades hit the "Holiday Inn" hotel. As you probably hear on the news, Sarajevo is without water, electricity, gas, telephones and food for a week now. Also the situation in general is getting worse and worse all the time, while the world is just watching all that disaster and agony of people, doing absolutely nothing to stop it or to help the people. The whole "civilized world" is supporting terror and massacre.

In the last fax which I received from Edina she tells me that Maja and Edvin can't bear it any longer. I feel so much helpless being here, and I wish I was with them all the time.

Try to send this fax which I just wrote to Edina. I'm not sure that you can, because they have no electricity and I do not know what's the situation with the fuel for the electric aggregate in the Ministry. But, please, try to get that fax through and if you do, let me know.

Love,

UP ALL NIGHT AGAIN, ERVIN?
FOR WEEKS I'VE SENT FAXES... TO POLITICIANS.. U.N. OFFICIALS... FRIENDS ... AGENCIES. TRYING SOME WAY TO GET THEM OUT. BUT...
...NO USE.

PROMISES... MAYBES... THAT'S ALL I GET.
THEY MEAN WELL... BUT... THAT DOESN'T HELP EDINA AND THE CHILDREN.

THE FAX IS NO HELP TO ME. I MUST ACT IN PERSON!

I WILL GO SEE THEM MYSELF. IN ROME. PARIS. AMSTERDAM. I WILL BEG ...ON MY KNEES...

I-I'LL NEED CAR-FARE, NEVEN. CAN YOU -
I'LL MAKE YOUR PLANE RESER-VATIONS, ERVIN.
I'M STILL A TRAVEL AGENT, YOU KNOW.

ROME, TWO DAYS LATER...
I WILL GO TO THE ITALIAN EMBASSY.
IF THEY GIVE PERMISSION... VISAS TO ENTER ITALY...
...EDINA AND THE KIDS WOULD BE ALLOWED TO LEAVE SARAJEVO.
2

AT A MINISTRY IN ROME...
I WOULD LIKE TO HELP YOU, MR. RUSTEMAGIC.
I AM ALSO AWARE YOU HAVE FRIENDS IN HIGH PLACES HERE IN ITALY. HOWEVER...

...WE ARE OVERWHELMED WITH REFUGEES FROM ALL OVER BOSNIA.
ITALY AND YUGOSLAVIA HAVE ALWAYS BEEN GOOD NEIGHBORS. BUT, NOW...
THANK YOU FOR YOUR TIME, SIR.

THE NEXT DAY, A JET DESCENDS TOWARDS ORLY AIRPORT...
TRAFFIC NEVER CHANGES IN PARIS.
THE FRENCH MINISTER OF HUMANITIES HAS AGREED TO SEE ME.

...AND YOU KNOW I WOULD DO IT... IF I COULD, ERVIN. BUT-
I KNOW, JACQUES.
I KNOW.

I HAVE ACCOMPLISHED NOTHING. I MUST GO BACK TO POREČ... AND THINK OF SOME OTHER WAY...

"...TO GET THEM OUT. HOW IT TEARS AT MY HEART. ARE THEY GETTING ENOUGH FOOD? WATER? ARE THEY ALL RIGHT?"
3

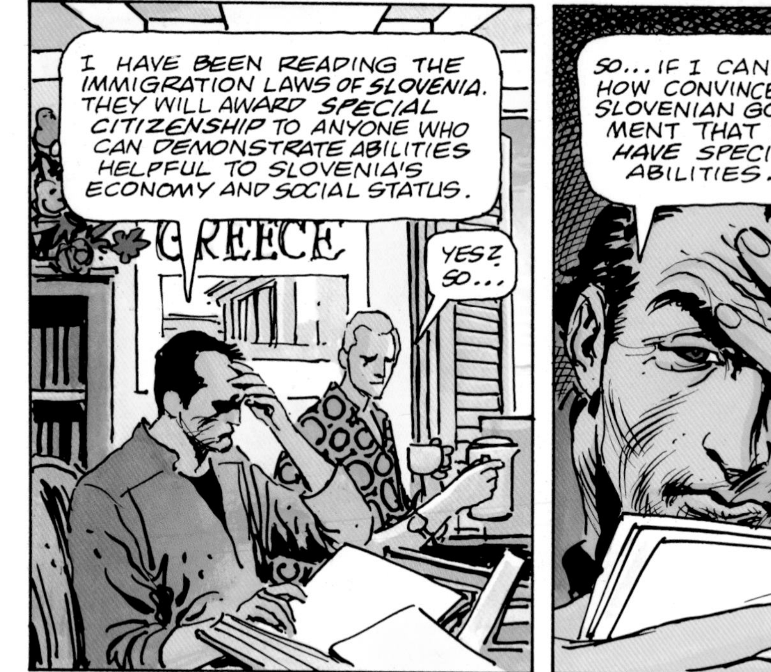

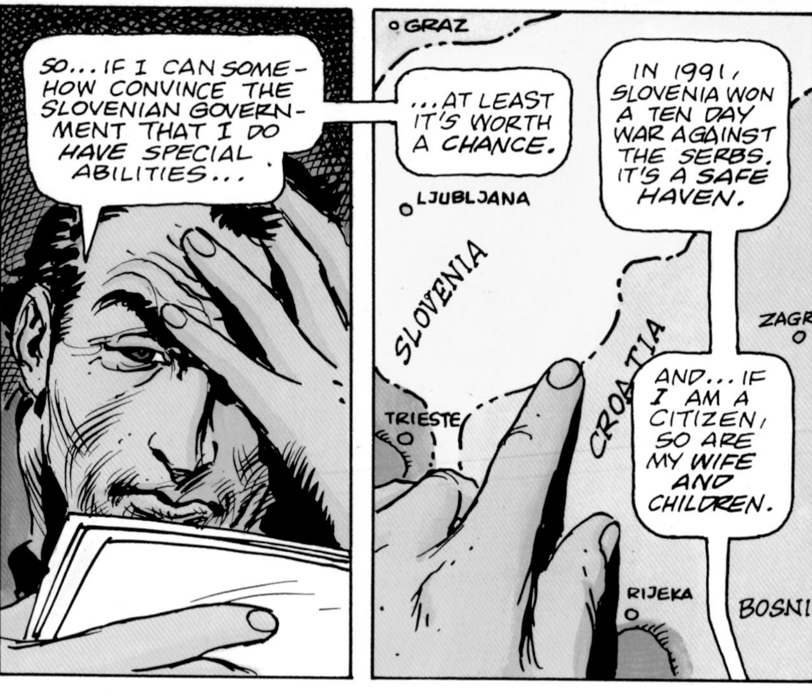

Porec (Istria), 23. 04. 1993

Dear Joe,

It was nice talking to you after such a long time. I'm sending you a model for the letter which I mentioned in our phone conversation.

You'll probably remember the apartment in Rome which Rinaldo Traini was offering to me some 9 months ago? Well, that place was already taken. However, now he has another place, which is a bit smaller, but which he is offering so generously to us, too.

I will be probably going to Rome on Wednesday/Thursday next week to see that place.

If you're faxing me back today, please address it to: Att: Neven (for Ervin). You remember Neven from Dubrovnik, I believe (?).

Love,

Ervin

IN SARAJEVO... AT THE HOLIDAY INN HOTEL...
LOOK, CHILDREN... PANCAKES. I FOUND SOME FLOUR... AND...
...I SAVED SOME POWDERED SUGAR...
I'M NOT HUNGRY, MAMA.
I... MISS PAPA.

I KNOW. I MISS HIM, TOO. BUT... HE IS WORKING TO GET US OUT.
AND YOU BOTH MUST BE STRONG... AND HEALTHY. READY TO LEAVE WHEN HE TELLS US. SO... EAT.
THE LEAVES ARE FALLING OFF THE TREES...
..THE WEATHER IS CHANGING.. BUT...
...I KNOW, DEAR ERVIN... THE SEASON DOES NOT SOFTEN THE PAIN FOR YOU... OR... FOR US.

AT THAT MOMENT IN POREČ...
YOU'RE UP EARLY, ERVIN. DID YOU SLEEP?
A LITTLE, NEVEN...
...IT'S DIFFICULT FOR ME TO SLEEP. EDINA MAY BE LOOKING AT THE SAME SKY... THINKING THE SAME THOUGHTS. SO NEAR... AND YET... SO FAR APART.

May 21, 1993

FROM: Ervin Rustemagic, Zagreb - Croatia - fax (38-41) 615-530

TO :

Dear Joe,

My friend in Zagreb is working together with the major organizer of convoys that evacuated people from Sarajevo last year.

They talked about my family today. He told him that he is preparing a new convoy for a long time now, but the organization is very difficult due to the current situation on the Bosnian ground, political problems etc. However, if there will be a convoy, they will take Edina, Maja and Edvin from Sarajevo.

Lots of love,

Ervin

Ervin Rustemagic

ZAGREB
DAYS LATER... ON THE ROAD BACK TO POREČ FROM ZAGREB...
POREČ
PAZIN
RIJEKA
IF NOTHING ELSE, THERE IS A CERTAIN NEGATIVE CONSISTENCY THAT CONTINUES TO AFFECT MY LIFE. I THOUGHT THERE WAS A CHANCE... BUT...
...THE MOTOR CONVOY LEFT SARAJEVO ...WITHOUT EDINA AND THE CHILDREN. I CANNOT STAND BEING AWAY FROM THEM. NOT KNOWING IF THEY ARE ALL RIGHT.
IN POREČ...
IT'S... NO USE. NOTHING IS WORKING. I'M GOING BACK! I WILL TELL NEVEN... AND TAKE THE FIRST FLIGHT BACK.
ERVIN! I'VE BEEN WAITING FOR YOU. AN OFFICIAL LETTER... FROM THE SLOVENIAN GOVERNMENT...
TH-THEY ARE AWARDING ME CITIZENSHIP IN SLOVENIA... AS A RESULT OF THE LETTERS OF RECOMMENDATION THEY RECEIVED FROM ALL OVER THE WORLD... FOR ME.
WON-DERFUL!
NOW... MY FAMILY WILL BE PERMITTED TO LEAVE BOSNIA. BECAUSE EDINA IS THE WIFE OF A SLOVENIAN CITIZEN.
PARIS

SARAJEVO...
...SEPTEMBER 25, 1993.
LIKE A SCENE FROM DANTE'S INFERNO, A PERPETUAL PALL OF SMOKE MANTLES THE ONCE-BEAUTIFUL CITY...
IT'S THE TELEPHONE, MAMA.
M-MAYBE IT'S... PAPA.

QUIET, CHILDREN.
HELLO? YES, YES... THIS IS EDINA RUSTEMAGIC. YES. I AM LISTENING...

WE ARE GOING TO BE WITH PAPA.

CHILDREN... WE MUST PACK ONLY WHAT WE CAN CARRY.
PAPA HAS MADE ARRANGEMENTS. HE WILL BE WAITING FOR US. TO MEET US.

THEY ARE SENDING A CAR TO PICK US UP... TO TAKE US TO THE AIRPORT. IN AN HOUR. WE MUST BE READY.
8

FROM: Ali Magnin / SAF B.V. Holland
TO: Joe/Muriel Kubert
DATE: April 29, 1993

FAX MESSAGE

Dear Joe/Muriel,

Ervin was in Zagreb for a few days to get visa for Italy. Yesterday afternoon he has flown to Split from where he will fly to Rome (Italy) this afternoon. Rinaldo offered him an apartment to stay in. We will try to get Dutch visas for the whole family, hoping that Edina and children will be evacuated very soon. Although, Ervin wrote that it seems to be very certain that the convoy for which Edina is planned will not go.

Best regards,

Ali

Porec (Croatia), May 14, 1993

Dear Scott,

I think I was very strong when I was in Sarajevo with my wife Edina and children, but since I left them there I had many passages of weaknesses and I became very sensitive. If something happens to them now I have nothing else to do but to commit a suicide. Therefore I'll have to go back to Sarajevo soon, unless I find a solution for their evacuation.

It is 27 days today since I left Sarajevo and I feel totally helpless, because I wasn't able to arrange anything for my family and myself. So, even if they get out from Bosnia soon, we don't have a place to go. I tried to get visas from several countries but without any success. The French turned us down right away although we have a welcome letter from their ex-minister. And even the Dutch rejected our request for visa in spite of the fact that I have an incorporated company in Holland. Nobody cares about the holders of Bosnian passports and we need visas for just every country we want to go to. I couldn't even get a permit for us to stay in Croatia (I'm illegally in Croatia now!). The visas for Italy don't exist and I managed to fly to Rome with two letters sent by publishers in Rome, stating that I'm invited there for business meetings. The customs' officer wanted to see my return air ticket and only after presenting such a ticket to him, I was allowed to enter the country and to stay there seven days maximum.

Also, it seems that the result of our attempt to get Slovenian passports and residence will be negative, though we didn't get a final answer yet. We collected some 25 letters from the publishers from all over the world and they will be seen by the president of their parliament in the next days. However, after a short period of optimism, I became a pessimist since I talked to some persons in Slovenia. Everybody said that we're at least 12 months late with our request, because the things have changed radically in that period. It looks like if the only chance is that we can get a transit visa for Slovenia only. Anyhow, I'll keep you posted how the things develop and what their final answer will be.

Love, Ervin

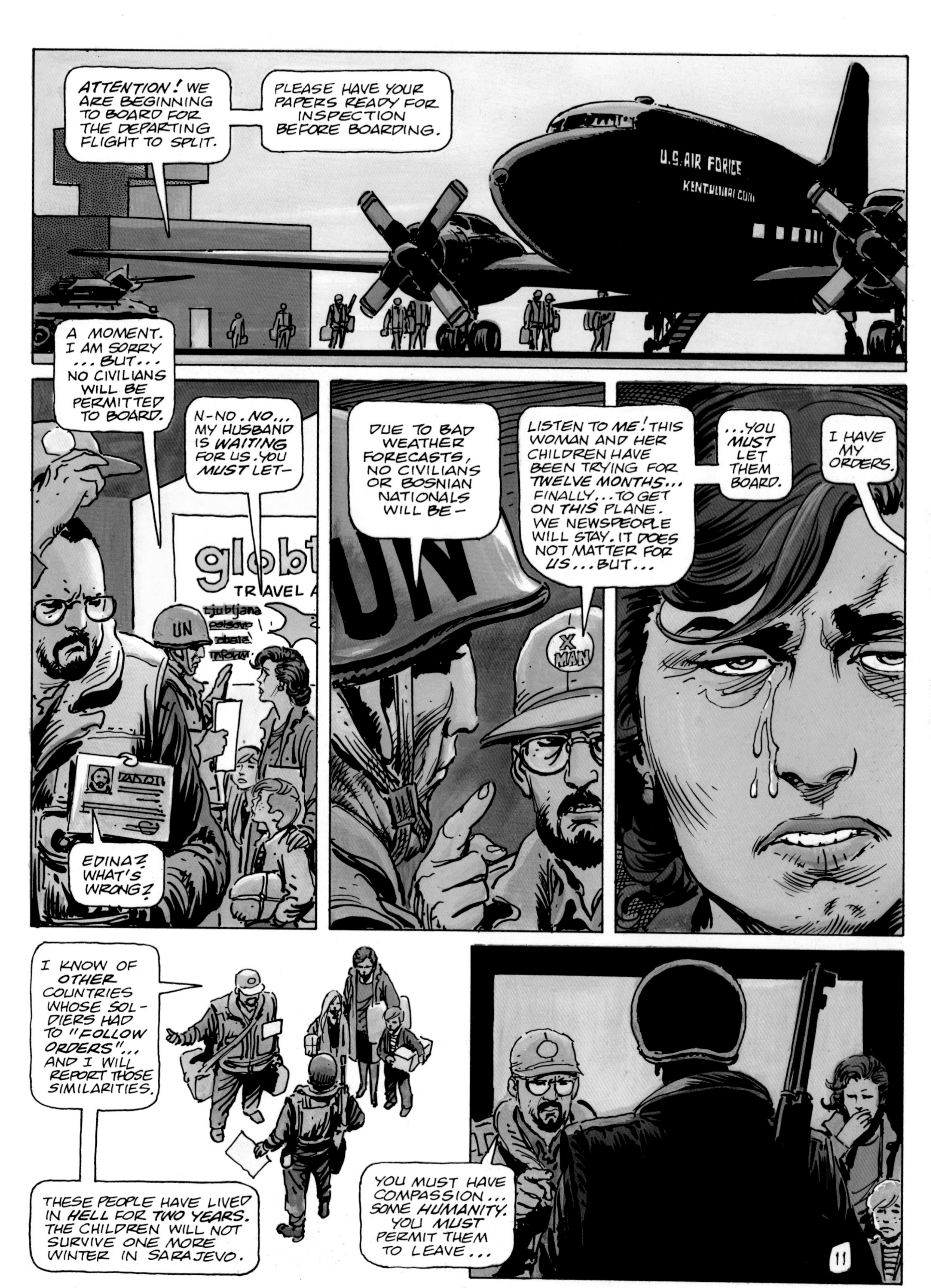
ATTENTION! WE ARE BEGINNING TO BOARD FOR THE DEPARTING FLIGHT TO SPLIT.
PLEASE HAVE YOUR PAPERS READY FOR INSPECTION BEFORE BOARDING.
U.S. AIR FORCE
A MOMENT. I AM SORRY ...BUT... NO CIVILIANS WILL BE PERMITTED TO BOARD.
N-NO. NO... MY HUSBAND IS WAITING FOR US. YOU MUST LET-
globt
TRAVEL A
Ljubljana
EDINA? WHAT'S WRONG?
DUE TO BAD WEATHER FORECASTS, NO CIVILIANS OR BOSNIAN NATIONALS WILL BE-
UN
LISTEN TO ME! THIS WOMAN AND HER CHILDREN HAVE BEEN TRYING FOR TWELVE MONTHS... FINALLY... TO GET ON THIS PLANE. WE NEWSPEOPLE WILL STAY. IT DOES NOT MATTER FOR US... BUT...
X MAN
...YOU MUST LET THEM BOARD.
I HAVE MY ORDERS.
I KNOW OF OTHER COUNTRIES WHOSE SOLDIERS HAD TO "FOLLOW ORDERS"... AND I WILL REPORT THOSE SIMILARITIES.
THESE PEOPLE HAVE LIVED IN HELL FOR TWO YEARS. THE CHILDREN WILL NOT SURVIVE ONE MORE WINTER IN SARAJEVO.
YOU MUST HAVE COMPASSION... SOME HUMANITY. YOU MUST PERMIT THEM TO LEAVE...
11

September 27, 1993

Dear Joe,

It was Saturday, September 25th, 1993, when I took an early morning flight from Zagreb to Split to welcome my family in Split, although I was not sure if they were going to come out that very day. There was a very strong wind in Split, and there were not many planes flying. Only the U.S. military aircrafts were operating. So, I was waiting at the Split airport with my friend, Nikola Listes. We couldn't know what was happening at the Sarajevo airport in the meantime.

Among the journalists there was also a German journalist Nigel Rahimpur. The funny thing was that I met Nigel in April, when he came to Sarajevo for the first time. And he came out from Sarajevo in April, together with me, on the same plane. And now, he is in Sarajevo for the second time in his life, and there he is, together with Edina and the kids. Around 1 P.M. the U.N. officer at the airport announced that they will be taken back to the city, because there will be no flights... Nigel started to yell for not taking this woman with two little children, who are waiting 12 months to get on the plane. These words stopped the captain and he decided to let them get aboard. They were the first civilians who were transported from Sarajevo, during the war, in the U.S. aircraft. Muriel said at that time that it did happen because 25th of September is a big Jewish holiday!... And, as you know, the great Rabin of Lubowitcher has given his blessing to Edina and the kids for a safe journey from Sarajevo. So, I was there, in Split, with my friend Nikola still waiting, but around 2 P.M. I was losing hope that they will come out that day. And the next plane landed. We saw one small child jumping on the ground. I couldn't recognize him, but I was hoping that it was Edvin. And then another, bigger child, jumped from the plane. It was Maja. Then we saw Edina... and both Nikola and myself started to cry and to hug each other. They were dressed in the same dresses which they had back in the winter, when we had tried to cross the runway of the Sarajevo airport. I was crying more and more... and now, I still have tears in my eyes.

Love, Ervin

ase dont excuse yourself for babbling hat babbling
s always very delighted to hear from you and as
ays very happy to answer your faxes but my problem
is that can hardly write he circumstances are such
t nothing functions normally here and just cannot
ncentrate to do anything at all lse it happens very
ten that after write a fax have to spend a few
rs trying to send it and cant get outside line on fax
phone ust be that people are telephoning so much to
h other that telephone lines just cant carry all these
ls lse now dont know whether ll be able to send
s fax to you or not

pril 12 1992

tell you that the situation is terrible or disastrous
ant tell you enough he situation is much worse than

last night was a very bad one as erbs were shelling
city the whole night hat part of the old city in
ch you and myself have walked is very much destroyed
he same thing with ostar serbs didnt destroy the
bridge yet but are intending to here is not much
lling during the day in arajevo but we hear shooting
the streets and it is very dangerous to walk or to
ve a car because the erbian terrorists are killing
ple from the roofs of high building mostly small
ldren using the rifles with sniperscopes

lease dont excuse yourself for babbli
delighted to hear from you and as alw
my problem now is that can hardly write
functions normally here and just cannot
it happens very often that after writ
trying to send it and cant get outside
are telephoning so much to each other t
these calls lse now dont know whethe
or not

f tell you that the situation is terr
enough he situation is much worse than

pril 12 1992

he last night was a very bad one as er
night hat part of the old city in which
much destroyed now he same thing with o
yet but are intending to here is not m
but we hear shooting in the streets and
a car because the erbian terrorists ar
building mostly small children using t
e just heard on the news that the nite
afternoon to take instant measures agai
and size of measures will be decided on
it to be fast but for us here two more
mean a period which is too long till w

which could write you longer than thi
it e live in such a way that we should
morning owever it is also difficult t
nights in the basement and were trying

lease send this fax to oe and uriel

ear oe

want you to know that we all citizens of arajevo
very very proud of our several hundred ewish citiz
r eresnjes the president of the ewish community i
arajevo was on our last night to tell the people
it is not true that they escaped from arajevo amel
all the erbian press radio and have published th
news on riday that all the ewish people have escap
from arajevo owever the erbian press and who a
under total control of ilosevic party are publishi
only lies and they are creating the news which suit
government
r eresnjes said that all the ewish citizens who a
able to work and fight will remain in arajevo to de
their city until the last of them lives

his statement produced tears in the eyes of all our
neighbors and all the people know in arajevo heref
wanted you to know that we all are very proud of t
f you could communicate this to the ewish communit
in your states perhaps they would send a nice note
encouragement to r eresnjes

he situation in osnia is very bad and is getting w
and worse every day he erbian terrorists supporte
the ugoslav ederal rmy are making massacres in sm
villages
especially along the river of rina which is dividi
osnia from erbia

oofs of the high buildings
iperscopes to kill people
of them were captured
t they were not shooting
erbian leaders are paying
shoot from the roof and

this and that the erbian
their and newspapers

note from the author

Having been a witness by fax to this incredible story, I felt compelled to record it in the best way I knew how. Despite the fact that "cartooning" and "comic books" have long been considered a child's medium here in the United States, I chose this means by which to communicate this story. It was a commitment I made to myself, while Ervin and his family were still trapped in the hell of Sarajevo. It was a promise to myself, that once they were out and safe, this is what I would do.

This story is true. The characters are real. I have taken certain liberties in creating dialogue, dramatizations, and variations of time sequences, in order to enhance (and in some cases, to curtail) the "storytelling" aspects of this book. However, in its essentials, the story adheres to fact. Some of the names are fictional, most are factual. If you feel, after reading, that this story is a stretch of the imagination, too much to be believed, I can fully understand the reaction. In reading and rereading Ervin's faxes (hundreds of them), I felt the same way. Nevertheless, this story *is* true.

e p i l o g u e

Many of the photographs of Sarajevo and environs that appear on the following pages were taken by Karim Zaimovic before his tragic death during the Bosnian War. The photos don't necessarily document the events detailed in the text portions of the epilogue, but serve as a small yet vivid legacy to Karim and to all the other thousands of Sarajevans to lose their lives in this senseless conflict.

There are additional photos taken by Ervin Rustemagic and others included here, showing, among other things, Ervin's family, the staff of the hospital in Dobrinja, and Joe and Muriel Kubert on vacation in Yugoslavia prior to the beginning of the war.

chapter 1

ervin returns to sarajevo

Ervin Rustemagic and I had known each other for at least twenty years. Our first meeting took place in Lucca, Italy, when I, for the first time, attended a European Cartoonists' Convention where Ervin also was present, having recently started his company Strip Art Features.

My wife Muriel and I visited him in Holland in early 1992. Ervin and I had agreed to work on some publishing projects together, and I had taken advantage of this trip to Europe to see him. Ervin's family, his wife Edina, daughter Maja, and son Edvin, were with him in Holland. The unrest in Sarajevo had already begun. As a precaution, Ervin had taken his family to Holland, where he maintained offices and an apartment. The family was in constant contact with Sarajevo, since Ervin's base was there. His main office, his home. His personnel continued to work while Ervin was away. And Ervin kept in touch and directed his operations from Holland.

In March 1992, things seemed to be quieting down in Sarajevo. Some sort of peace seemed imminent, and optimistic headlines reflected these hopes.

Edina and the children were becoming terribly homesick. After all, they were born and raised in Sarajevo, as was Ervin. Edina's family was still there, as were Edvin's and Maja's school chums and friends. They were homesick. School was already starting, and the language barrier (Dutch is completely dissimilar from Croatian) made it even more difficult for the kids to assimilate.

A week after our visit with the Rustemagics, we left Europe for home. Back in the States, we received a fax from Ervin that Edina and the kids had returned to Sarajevo. This, despite his exhortations not to go, and the words of concern expressed by Muriel when she spoke to Edina in Holland while I was busy with Ervin. A short while later, Ervin followed his family. Within days of his arrival in Sarajevo, the war escalated to the degree that no longer could anyone walk the streets of Sarajevo, much less attempt to leave the city. The war had begun in earnest.

Photos: Scenes in Sarajevo during the war (p. 184); Ervin Rustemagic's family (p. 185).

chapter 2

war is hell!

It soon became apparent via Ervin's faxes that the war in Bosnia-Herzegovina was *not* a war between armies to be fought on military battlefields, but to be waged on the streets of cities and towns and directed specifically at civilians.

Children were selected targets. Serb snipers were paid a bonus per target's head. Children were selected for mercenary reasons. When a child was hit, his parents would run out to get him. To bring him to safety. This afforded the sniper a double bonus, at least. The child *and* those who came out to help.

Ervin's home in Dobrinja, a suburb of Sarajevo, was not far from the emergency hospital just a few blocks away. The hospital was set up in what was originally a supermarket situated on the base floor of a substantial stone and brick building. Outside, sandbags stacked six to eight feet high protected the plate-glass windows. A tattered, white flag emblazoned with a red cross identified the new use within.

All about him, the people of Sarajevo attempted to adapt to a nightmare that had befallen them. Ervin maintained his publishing work schedule as best he could under these incredibly difficult circumstances, and in this way, retained some semblance of normalcy. Meanwhile, Ervin's friends on the outside were in constant contact by fax with him and each other. Despite interruptions of electricity, faxes were received and sent via satellite transmission.

In the United States and the rest of the world, television and newspapers were beginning to report the atrocities occurring in Bosnia-Herzegovina. Almost like an echo of the terrible events of World War II. But, no, that *couldn't* be possible. The world would not *allow* that horror to happen again.

On April 15, 1992, an editorial in the *New York Times* appeared with the headline "Stop the Butcher of the Balkans." It described Slobodan Milosevic, the Serbian leader, as one who "has wheeled and lashed out mercilessly at Muslim-majority towns in Bosnia. From the hillsides, Serb irregulars, backed by the Serb-led remnants of the Yugoslav army, indiscriminately blast round after round into Bosnia's defenseless communities."

Photos: Scenes in Sarajevo (p. 186), Edvin Rustemagic (p. 186, bottom right); scenes in Sarajevo (p. 187)

chapter 3

life in sarajevo

* * *

edvin is ill

More and more stories emanated from what was once the nation of Yugoslavia concerning the abuse of civilians and the merciless destruction of cities and towns. The term "war crimes" was seen more and more often in newspaper articles and heard on TV reports.

The old bridge in Mostar, a span that stood for hundreds of years, had been destroyed. Bombed out of existence. Four years before, Muriel and I, accompanied by Ervin, had walked along that bridge into the beautiful city of Mostar. We were on our way to Dubrovnik on the southern shore of the Adriatic Sea. The country had seemed so beautiful and peaceful then.

Now, each new fax from Ervin described the increasing escalation of the war.

"April 21, 1992: We're still alive, although there is enormous shooting very close to this area . . . Serbian's specialty is to come into peoples' homes, kill, and steal all valuable things . . . "

Invariably, the news we got from Ervin's faxes came days before the same reports were received from our local newspapers and TVs. Our friend and his family were in the middle of it.

When Ervin told us of his son Edvin's illness, I could only imagine the fear and frustration he and Edina must have suffered. A sick child. Little, if any, medicine. A step outside their house invited a shell or a bullet. And yet, through it all, the family pushed and pulled, wept and grimaced. After all, what choice did they have?

Ervin asked us to fax any U.S. newspaper articles, including photos, concerning reportage on Sarajevo and Bosnia-Herzegovina. These he supplied to newspapers in Sarajevo, which had been diminished to only a few pages but still continued to be published. It was important for them to know that those on the outside were aware. Aware and they cared.

Photos: Joe and Muriel Kubert vacationing in Yugoslavia prior to the war (p. 188); Edvin Rustemagic (p. 189, top), scenes in Sarajevo (p. 189)

AUTO
SERVIS

chapter 4

ervin's place is destroyed * * * they run

All of us, all of Ervin's friends on the outside, used whatever contacts and influence we had to gain an exit for the Rustemagics. Politicians, religious organizations, business executives, governmental agencies. We wrote letters, telephoned, sent urgent faxes, all to little avail. They *wanted* to help, but the Rustemagics were only one family among thousands who were in the same terrible position.

I remember Ervin telling me that during the first month of his return to Sarajevo, he was in a state of constant fear during the incessant bombing and shelling. He knew that any one of those detonations could mean a bloody end to his family and himself. Then, he said, a strange thing happened. The steady rain of eruptions became accepted. Almost a norm. When he began making nightly runs to the hospital, in order to help any way he could, sometimes Ervin actually *hoped* for the eruption of a grenade. Nights were so dark and the streets so littered with wreckage and abandoned vehicles that only the momentary flash of a shell's detonation kept him from collisions that might have broken his leg or skull. Of course, he would take precautions, such as not promenading along "Sniper Alley" (outside the Holiday Inn Hotel) and keeping the family in the middle of their apartment rather than near the windows. "Amazing how adaptable we humans are," he said.

The day that the Serb tank rumbled up his street, the war had come to his very doorway. The family ran, Ervin clutching Edvin to his chest. Edina and Maja ran beside him, as the tank's cannon obliterated every vestige of house, home and business. Ervin, Edina, and the children had been caught in the suction created by the vacuum of "ethnic cleansing." A particle of dust in the mounting debris.

In the twenty or so years I have known Ervin, I never knew that he was of Muslim heritage. And he readily admits that he never felt himself a Muslim per se. He was a citizen of Sarajevo. All his life he had lived beside Turks and Indians, Serbs and Jews, without any hint of animosity or discomfort. Jews, in particular, had found the city of Sarajevo a refuge. An exception from most of the rest of Europe. Now, as a result of a war foisted on people by power-hungry leaders, Ervin discovered his ethnicity. Now, people who were once considered friends and neighbors were bent on the annihilation of his family. *Ethnic cleansing*. A euphemism for *mass murder*.

Having been born and raised in Sarajevo, and having operated his business only a few blocks from his home, Ervin knew the city and its environs well. When the tank's cannon blasted his home to rubble, he led his family to the apartments vacated by friends. Sarajevo had become a city of refugees, where frightened occupants ran to exchange places with other frightened occupants, who ran to a supposedly safer place. In so doing, a child's toy or a family picture was left behind. Too much to carry in a need to move quickly. Leftovers. A mute introduction to the new tenants who would (too soon) be on the move themselves. Musical chairs, accompanied by explosions.

Photos: Scenes in Sarajevo (p. 190-191)

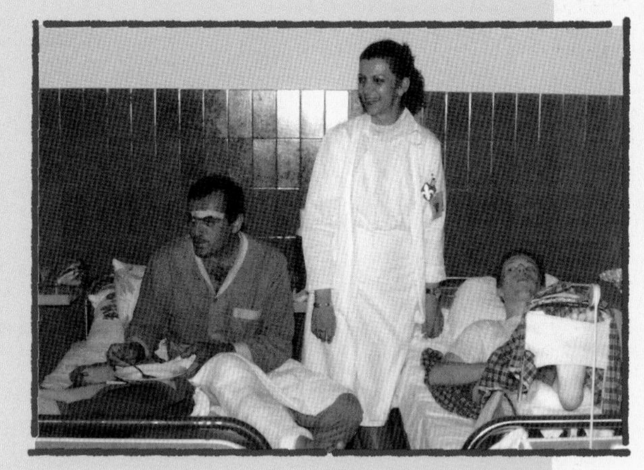

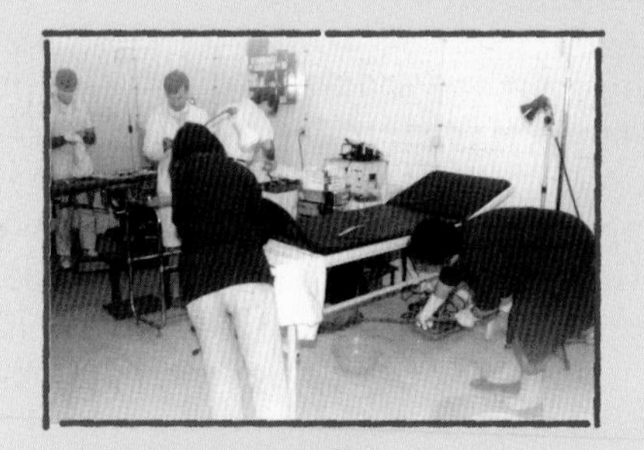

chapter 5

the run to sarajevo

In June 1992, Ervin could feel the tempo of the war continue to increase. At times, a deafening crescendo. The devastation was everywhere. Civilians who dared walk the streets to find water from the broken mains became bloody, broken bits of humanity, victims of shells or grenades.

Ervin came to know the doctors and nurses at the nearby emergency hospital. He was witness to the pain and suffering of the people brought in. Men, women, and little children, with missing arms and legs. Torn bodies. Somewhere, he found a video camera and filmed footage of excruciating civilian suffering in a country gone mad. Later, on the tape he sent us, we saw the indescribable.

He gave his car (an Opel Kadet) to the doctors, to be used as an ambulance. And, miracle of miracles, the hospital possessed an emergency generator by which a fax machine could operate. This enabled Ervin to communicate with his friends on the outside. The satellite fax at the Ministry in Sarajevo was also available for Ervin's use.

So far, the family was intact. Except for Edvin's short illness and the emotional effect on Edina and Maja, they had been lucky. So far. But how long would their luck last? They had to get out of Sarajevo. Ervin knew that any opportunity to leave Sarajevo would necessitate getting first from the suburb of Dobrinja, then into Sarajevo proper. They had to be near the Ministry, where official permission to leave might be given. To do this, they had to run an extremely dangerous passage between Dobrinja and the city proper.

On the road from Dobrinja to the city of Sarajevo, there was a row of twenty or thirty derelict vehicles, behind which Serb units set up fixed, heavy-caliber machine guns aimed at anything that attempted passage. And from the hills, the city of Sarajevo itself was under constant siege, completely surrounded by Serb forces.

Protected from machine-gun bullets by magazines and comic books, Ervin made his first, white-knuckled, teeth-clenched trip into the city in his ambulance-converted Opel. Like a pony express rider racing through the attacking Indians. Every day, many who attempted that ride were either killed or wounded. *Many.* Miraculously, despite the number of trips he made, he remained unscratched. Unharmed.

Photos: Ervin Rustemagic (left) with the staff at the hospital in Dobrinja (p. 192); two members of the hospital staff with "ambulance" (p. 193, top), scenes in Sarajevo (p. 193)

PAZI ↑
RUŠI SE

chapter 6

the birthday party

It has been stated and validated that not one window in the entire city of Sarajevo remained uncracked or unbroken. Not one building was left unscathed from grenades and bullets. Ervin continued to make his dangerous run into the city for a number of reasons. He had to keep in touch with the Ministry, in the event permission was finally given for them to emigrate. It was essential to stay in physical contact with those who might be able to help. And he was thereby able to utilize another source of sending and receiving faxes, through the satellite fax machine in the Ministry building.

Maja's tenth birthday was celebrated at this time. Knowing that Maja loved Barbie dolls, my wife faxed several pages of a Barbie comic book to the Rustemagics, as a birthday present for Maja. She received them and later told us how much she enjoyed them.

The courage of the ravaged people of Sarajevo has become legend. Radio transmission had been drastically curtailed, but still, the station operated. As did the TV and the newspaper. *Oslobodjenje*, the local paper, was sometimes reduced to a single, folded sheet. But still, they published.

In the midst of all this death and destruction, Ervin took advantage of any opportunity that might help them get out. Disregarding the dangers, he moved through places he knew had been occupied by people who no longer survived this awful onslaught. People who had lost limbs and lives. Saw their loved ones torn from their very grasp. His faxes reflected his growing cynicism.

Later, Ervin said, "What else could I do? If I had crawled into a hole with my family, that would've been the end for us all. I had no choice."

Ervin had learned that his mother, who had a home outside the city, had become ill and had been taken to a hospital. Eventually, he was told that her home had been destroyed, and that she had been killed when the hospital was captured by the Serbs.

Photos: Scenes in Sarajevo (p. 194); Ervin Rustemagic and family (p. 195, 2nd from top), scenes in Sarajevo (p. 195)

SARAJEVO
ULAZ
ZLATNI RESTORAN
GALLERY
UN

chapter 7
the rape camp

Until now, Ervin had been driving past the gauntlet of trucks in Sarajevo by himself. But now, he had to consider the trip accompanied by Edina and the children. It was an awful decision to make. To put his wife and children to the extreme in harm's way. I've often wondered what I would have done under those conditions. Could any of us know how we would react placed in a similar situation?

More revelations of atrocities committed against the civilian population began to surface in news reports worldwide. Of rape camps in which women (mothers, wives, sisters, children) were incarcerated and abused, with the purpose of bearing Serb children. Another method of "ethnic cleansing." Whole villages were scourged. All males were put into concentration camps. Evidence of beatings and starvation appeared in clandestine photographs taken at these various sites. Ervin's resolve to leave Sarajevo was enforced by these events.

As they prepared to leave Dobrinja for the city, Edina's father, who lived close by, paid them a visit. He had learned of their plans and wanted to see the family for perhaps the last time. No, he would not leave Sarajevo.

The description of the old man leaving the Rustemagics' apartment in Dobrinja was told to me by Ervin, as we sat in a small restaurant in lower Manhattan in early 1995. As Ervin spoke, I could envision the old man crossing the street, waving back to the family and the shell landing close by the old man's feet. And Edina's reaction, first that her father had been killed, then of his incredible escape from injury.

Ervin spoke of the emergency lamps the people assembled for the times that the electricity was disrupted. A glass or jar half-filled with cooking oil with a cork floating on its surface. A shoelace or cord is passed through the cork. A wick. The rest of the lace/cord dangles below, in the oil. The wick is lit, supplying light.

Transistor radios became useless when their batteries died, and replacement batteries were not available. By hooking wires from the telephone outlet to the radio, the transistor radio became operable.

Photos: Scenes in Sarajevo (p. 196-197)

Holiday Inn
HOTEL

СВЈЕТЛОСТ

SARAJEVO
SIGURAVA IMOVINU

chapter 8

new tenants at the holiday inn

Ervin's decision to bring Edina and the children into the city of Sarajevo was made for him. He had received word from the Ministry that arrangements were in effect for the family to leave. They had to be available at a moment's notice.

This, however, turned out to be only one of a series of heartbreaking disappointments for the Rustemagics. The plans for their evacuation fell through. They had to find a place to stay. They couldn't go back to Dobrinja. They had said their good-byes, and their apartment had been occupied by another homeless family almost immediately.

Ervin persuaded the manager of the Holiday Inn Hotel in Sarajevo to give them a room. You must understand how difficult an accomplishment that was.

In addition to the extremely high rental charge, the rooms were at a premium. Every newspaper, magazine, and television company in the world had their representatives in Sarajevo to cover the war. Top reporters and commentators from every country. And, it seemed, they all had reservations at the Holiday Inn Hotel.

Ervin never stopped trying to get out. Despite the failed promises and his mounting cynicism, he knew that the lives of his wife and children were at constant risk. Later, Ervin commented, "It was like being on a roller coaster. For a minute, things looked good. As if we had a chance. The next, down into the dumps."

The chilling reality of someone sacrificing themselves for a cigarette was an example of how the value of life itself had deteriorated. Almost meaningless. Smoking, indeed, was harmful to one's health.

Photos: Scenes in Sarajevo (p. 198), Maja Rustemagic with friend (p. 198, 2nd right from top); scenes in Sarajevo (p. 199)

chapter 9

attempt to cross the airport

While his friends were trying their best to solicit aid through every possible means, Ervin was sending faxes back and forth across oceans and continents. But he was becoming more and more convinced that their salvation lay with themselves. And that they, the family, would have to dare even more extreme dangers if they were ever to get out of Sarajevo.

Many people were aware of the escape route across the airfield on the outskirts of Sarajevo. It was no secret. Night after night, shadowy figures scurried back and forth under the noses of Serb gunners and U.N. soldiers alike. A cross-traffic was created by citizens, bringing contraband food and materials into the city, passing those attempting to escape the city. The perilous trip across the airfield was only the first step in this dangerous escape route. Once having gotten to the far-side, chain-link fence of the airport, the evacuees would then have to walk many miles across mountainous, snow-covered terrain, through the winter night, to the relatively safe town of Pazaric. Every path and road was mined. The Rustemagics were ill-clothed for the trip. The children were wearing light sneakers and summer jackets.

Borne by fear and desperation, the attempt was made. Although unsuccessful, the fact the family returned uninjured was a miracle itself.

Meanwhile, Ervin's friends continued to explore other avenues of escape. Vivid newspaper accounts substantiated by Ervin's tense faxes described a situation that was becoming more dangerous for them with every passing day.

Photos: Scenes in Sarajevo (p. 200-201)

SA 272775

UN

chapter 10

the soldier of fortune

The war did not diminish. Serb forces in the mountains surrounding the city increased their long-range cannon fire without interruption. Thousands upon thousands of civilian casualties were recorded. A youngster who disregarded the constant warnings of elders in a desire to behave more like a normal child in play, outside in the sun and snow, could become one of the missing the next day.

Despite Ervin's attempts to be upbeat in his faxes, we could tell that his morale was hitting rock bottom. And why not? Promises from foreign government officials, in Sarajevo and elsewhere, were consistent in only one aspect. Each resulted in failures of completion. Ervin pursued all avenues, no matter how flimsy the chance. And so did his friends on the outside.

Martin Lodewijk in Dordrecht, Holland, had somehow become aware of a man who said he had recently been in Sarajevo. The man described himself as someone with the ability to enter and leave the city at will. Yes, he had also helped others to escape, and, for a price, could and would do it for Ervin.

There was no way to check the man's story or his credentials, nor was there time to do so. This was only a possibility, but one that could not be ignored.

Ervin and his family's situation was becoming desperately critical. Only a matter of time until his luck would run out.

Arrangements were made. Monies were paid. But soon after having received the requested funds, the soldier of fortune disappeared. Enriched, apparently, by the dollars he was to use to get the Rustemagics out of Sarajevo.

Disappointed but undeterred, Ervin implemented another plan.

If he could gain official accreditation as a newspaper or television correspondent, he could receive official sanction to leave Sarajevo. Newspeople had complete freedom to enter and leave the war-ravaged city at will. Once outside, he would move heaven and earth to get Edina and the children out. Ervin faxed his friends, who then set in motion his plan to acquire the accreditation he needed.

Time moved slowly. Months passed, but eventually Ervin received documentation as a newsman for a foreign TV station. Arrangements were made for his departure. Even to the point of getting to the airport terminal and waiting to board the aircraft outside. Then, another disappointment. At the last minute, the flight was called off.

Photos: Scenes in Sarajevo (p. 202-203)

G.B.

chapter 11

ervin gets out

The up-and-down roller coaster continued to rule the lives of the Rustemagics. Finally, despite Ervin's feeling that his bad luck would never change, he was airborne on a French military aircraft, leaving Sarajevo.

His first destination was Split, a city on the coast of the Adriatic. Upon landing, he telephoned his friends to notify them of his escape. He spent his first night of freedom in Split. The next day, he left for Rijeka, and thence to Porec.

Uppermost in his mind was getting Edina and the children out. Toward this end, Ervin traveled back and forth to Zagreb, Rome, Split, and other places, borrowing money for train, bus, and air flights. He spoke to government officials, acquaintances, anyone who would listen. But everywhere he turned, he came up against a stone wall.

Now, the situation struck him full force. *He* was out, but Edina, Maja, and Edvin were still in there. In the Hell Hole. At any moment, a bomb or bullet could spell disaster for his family, and he could do nothing to help them. Only a few hundred miles away, yet he was helpless to do anything for them. Ervin made up his mind then that if he could not get his family out, *he* would return to Sarajevo. Better to be *with* them than to be apart like this. Against all protestations by his friends, his mind was made up. Edina had learned of his decision and faxed him that he must *not* return. If he did, they would lose any chance of ever getting out of the besieged and battered city.

For Ervin, her words were the most persuasive. He was now more determined than ever to secure safe exit for his wife and children.

Photos: Scenes in Sarajevo (p. 204); Maja and Edvin Rustemagic (p. 205, 2nd from top), scenes in Sarajevo (p. 205)

chapter 12

edina and the kids get out

Ervin's every waking thought was of Edina, Maja, and Edvin. As possibilities for arranging the family's departure arose, they were crushed again and again. Ervin continued to travel all over the continent in his vain attempts to extricate them. But the continual stream of failures was causing his resolve to crumble. He gave himself a deadline of just a few days more, after which he would return to Sarajevo. Nothing could deter him. His mind was made up.

Then it happened.

One of Ervin's ideas had been to apply to the neighboring country of Slovenia for special citizenship. Ervin had learned that under certain unique circumstances, Slovenia would accept an immigrant from a foreign country. He mounted a campaign, encouraged his friends worldwide to send letters of recommendation to the government of Slovenia attesting to Ervin's past history as a successful and honorable businessman, and that he would be a unique asset to that country. Although he held little optimism for his plan's success, Ervin knew that if he could gain citizenship in Slovenia, his wife and children would also become citizens, and therefore be permitted to leave Sarajevo.

Then, word came that he had indeed been granted citizenship in Slovenia. The next step was to get the family out.

Within days, Edina was notified at the Holiday Inn that she and the children could "leave Sarajevo whenever you are ready."

On the morning of September 25, 1993, Ervin was at the airport in Split, waiting for the arrival of his wife and children. He was unaware of the drama that was taking place in the Sarajevo airport at that very moment.

All those waiting for the flight from Sarajevo to Split were told that no one would be permitted to board except military personnel. The U.S. military air transport, the *Kentucky Air Guard*, would not carry *any* civilians. This included Edina, the children, and several news correspondents.

Incredibly, one of the German newspaper correspondents had flown with Ervin when he left Sarajevo months earlier. They had been friends prior to the war. The reporter had returned to Sarajevo and was now on his way back to Split.

The reporter recognized Edina and was witness to the taut situation taking place. Immediately, he spoke to the U.N. officer and argued the injustice and sheer cruelty of these actions. Perhaps it was the reporter's emotional response. Or the expressions on the faces of the children. Moments later, Edina, Edvin, and Maja were permitted to board the plane. None of the reporters were allowed that privilege and had to remain in Sarajevo.

Meanwhile, Ervin was waiting at the airport in Split, not knowing if his family was actually en route, or if they would ever arrive. Was this going to be like all the other times? All the other disappointments? Then, there it was. The *Kentucky Air Guard*, descending through the clouds. Landing.

The rear hatch swung open. Suddenly, two small figures were running toward him. They were really here. Amidst hugging and kissing and tears of joy, the family was safe . . . and together.

Photos: Scenes in Sarajevo (p. 206), Maja and Edvin Rustemagic (p. 206, 3rd right from top); scenes in Sarajevo (p. 207)